Aircraft & Legend
FOCKE - WULF
Fw 190 & Ta 152

HEINZ J. NOWARRA

Foulis

Haynes

A **FOULIS** Aviation Book

First published 1987 in German by Motorbuch Verlag as 'Focke-Wulf Fw 190-Ta 152'
by Heinz J. Nowarra

English language edition published 1988
Reprinted 1989

Published by:
Haynes Publishing Group
Sparkford, Nr. Yeovil, Somerset BA22 7JJ,
England

Haynes Publications Inc.
861 Lawrence Drive, Newbury Park,
California 91320, USA

British Library Cataloguing in Publication Data
Nowarra, Heinz J. (Heinz Joachim), *1912-*
    Focke Wulf FW109-Ta152.
    1. Focke-Wulf FW109 aeroplanes, 1937-1945
    I. Title
    623.74'64
    ISBN 0-85429-695-6

Library of Congress catalog card number 88-80558

Editor: Mansur Darlington
Cover illustration: David Parker
Translator: Ian Gordon
Printed in England by: J.H. Haynes & Co. Ltd

Contents

Introduction

In 1964 I was commissioned by English publishers to write a book on the Fw 190. Thanks to Eberhard Weber and Helmut Roosenboom, both at VFW-Bremen, I was given access to the old Focke-Wulf Archive material on the Fw 190. Herr Weber assisted my work by providing information from these archives. The result was the book entitled *The Focke-Wulf, a Famous German Fighter.* Over the last 20 years, however, a considerable amount of fresh material had come to light, so it was time to produce a new and updated book. I am grateful to Motorbuch-Verlag [the book's original German publisher] for their decision to publish this book.

I have made every effort to investigate all the sources available to me and to create the most complete overview of all the prototypes and series designs of the Fw 190 and its successor the Ta 152. This would have been impossible without the help of others.

In particular I should like to acknowledge the assistance of Gebhard Aders, Helmut Roosenboom, Peter Petrick, Fritz Trenkle, H.P. Dabrowski, Carl Hildebrandt, Jay P. Spenser of the National Air and Space Museum, Smithsonian Institution, and especially the VFW-Bremen Works of Messerschmitt-Bölkow-Blohm.

The loss of most of the original German documents means that a totally error-free, exhaustive account of the history of this oustanding aircraft is probably not feasible, but I hope I have succeeded in providing the enthusiast with the most accurate picture possible of the Fw 190/Ta 152.

Heinz Nowarra

1. The Birth of the Focke-Wulf Fw 190

It was the last week of July 1937. The whole world gasped in amazement at the success of German aircraft in the Zurich Air Races – especially the German Messerschmidt Bf 109 Fighter. But in the Reichsluftfahrtministerium (German Air Ministry) people were asking whether the choice of the Bf 109 as the *only* German Luftwaffe standard fighter was not a mistake. The Technisches Amt (Technical Office of the German Air Ministry) and the Inspektion der Jagdflieger (Fighter Inspectorate) could not agree. They also discussed the fact that no decision had been taken for the Luftwaffe to be restricted to a single fighter type.

In England there was the Spitfire in addition to the Hurricane. In France both the Morane 406 and the Bloch 150 were being built, and in Italy the old Fiat CR 32, the rather better G 50 and the new Macchi MC 200 fighter all existed in parallel.

The discussions continued until the Spring of 1938. Then the Technisches Amt decided to invite tenders for a second fighter aircraft. It was assumed that the prototype would require 12 to 18 months development. Lead time to production was usually in the order of two years at that time so the new fighter would not be ready for service use until 1941 at the earliest and so would certainly need a more powerful engine than the Daimler-Benz DB 600 or DB 601 currently being produced. The only more powerful engine which was at all suitable was the 14-cylinder twin-row BMW 139 which would produce 1500 PS instead of the 1100 PS of the DB 601. The BMW 189 had been on the test bench since the Spring of 1937 and nine of these engines were built and tested successfully, but development was still incomplete.

There was considerable surprise in the Summer of 1938 when the construction of a pre-production series for a fighter of this type was allocated. It was awarded to Focke-Wulf, as Messerschmidt were already working to capacity with the Bf 109, and Dornier, Heinkel and Junkers were assigned to the construction of bombers and naval aircraft. There was spare production capacity at Focke-Wulf who had taken over the old Albatros Works in Berlin-Johannisthal. Professor Focke, who together with Georg Wulf had founded the company and had been its Technical Director, had now turned his attention to building helicopters. His successor was Kurt Tank, a man who had proved his worth at Rohrbach, and already had a number of successful designs at Focke-Wulf to his credit.

In the meantime things had been happening in the aircraft engine world which were destined to influence the development of the new fighter. In June 1938 negotiations began between BMW (Bayerische Motorenwerke) and the Brandenburgische Motorenwerke (part of the Siemens organisation) and led to a BMW takeover one year later.

In the meantime development of the new fighter started at Focke-Wulf in July 1938 under the direction of Kurt Tank. Realisation of the project was under the control of Oberingenieur Mittelhuber, who was working to a design by Oberingenieur Willy

Kurt Tank, the father of the Fw 190

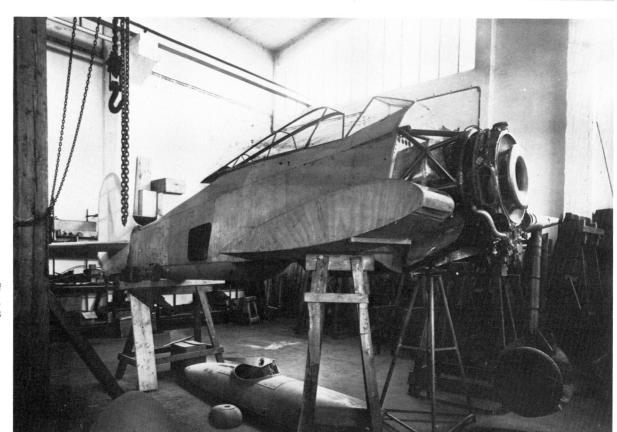

Wooden mock-up of the new fighter, Autumn 1938

8

Focke-Wulf Fw 190 V1, the first prototype, nearing completion, Spring 1939

Käther. The detailed design work was the responsibility of a design group led by Oberingenieur Blaser. Little did Blaser realise that this work would later take him to the very brink of physical and mental breakdown. The new aircraft was given the designation Focke-Wulf Fw 190. As all previous Focke-Wulf aircraft had been named after birds such as *Habicht* (Hawk) and *Möwe* (Seagull), the Fw 190 was also named after a bird: *Würger* (shrike or butcher bird).

Blaser now set to work systematically, but suddenly the Technisches Amt demanded that work on the Fw 190 should be speeded up, presumably at the instigation of the Generalstab (general staff). It is reasonable to assume they were already aware of Hitler's warlike intentions. The deadlines set for Blaser were so tight that he moved his bed to an office and worked there tirelessly day and night. The frenzied activity of Blaser and his team was not without success, for the prototype Fw 190 V1

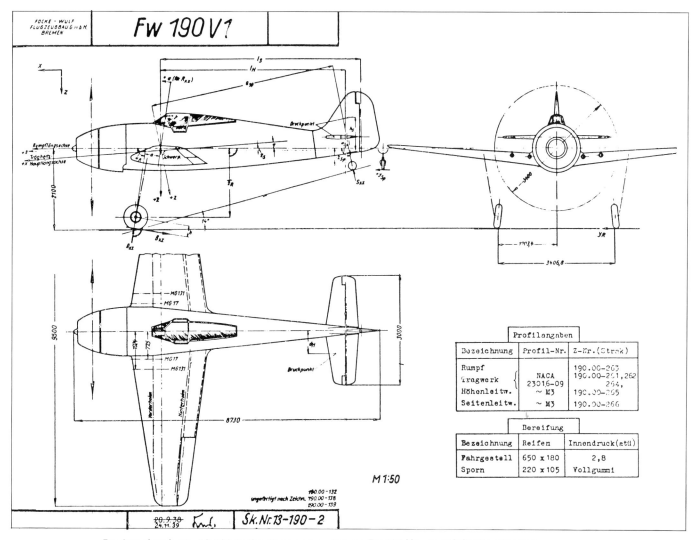

Design sketch no. 13-190-2: the shape of prototype Fw 190 V1, as originally planned

Fw 190 V1 shortly before its first flight, May 1939 still without registration numbers

(Versuchsflugzeug 1) was rolled out of the hangar at the end of May 1939. Sander, the chief test pilot who was to remain in charge of test-flying the Fw 190 and its successor the Ta 152 right up to the end of the war, flew the Fw 190 V1 on its maiden flight on 1 June 1939.

In comparison with the Messerschmidt Bf 109, the Fw 190 V1 looked very chunky because of its radial engine and it had been given a spinner which was so large that its outer edge was faired flush with the engine cowling. The air-cooled radial engine was cooled through the hollow centre of the spinner.

We must assume that the maiden flight by Sander was successful as Blaser (who was suffering from severe exhaustion) collapsed through sheer relief. He was immediately sent to a sanatorium to convalesce. The food there was so bad, however, that he

preferred to return to his work in Bremen. In fact the food in the military factories was considerably better; not only did the workers there get additional food ration cards, but also very good canteen food, whereas in the sanatorium Blaser would only have received normal rations. His behaviour was interpreted as passive resistance to the Nazi regime and he received severe warnings as a result. It was only with great difficulty that he succeeded in explaining that he had left the sanatorium purely to regain his health and return to work as quickly as possible.

Right from the very first flight Sander had established that the BMW 139 engine did not meet the specifications and was unreliable.

Fw 190 V1 was given the civil aviation markings D-OPZE and transferred to Rechlin to the Luftwaffe Test Centre. There it was flown by three test pilots, Diplom Ingenieur Francke, Dipl.Ing. Beauvais and Dipl.Ing.

Thoenes. All three of them confirmed that the aircraft handled extremely well, but they did complain that the engine overheated. In July Generalluftzeugmeister General Udet (General of Air Equipment, Luftwaffe) and Generalingenieur Lucht (Luftwaffe Chief Engineer) visited Rechlin to check on the development of the Fw 190. They were more than somewhat surprised when Francke welcomed them wearing summer clothing and shorts. He was backed up by the other two test pilots when he explained that although the machine did fly well it was desperately hot in the cockpit, so the pilot was forced to fly in shirtsleeves and shorts. Consequently Blaser had to change the engine installation in the second prototype Fw 190 V2, FO + LZ, so that a cooling fan could be incorporated to reduce the temperature of the BMW 139.

When the second prototype (V2) with the new cooling arrangements flew for the first time on 30 November 1939 and without them on 6 and 9 December, it became apparent that this attempt at a solution was totally unsatisfactory. It was also discovered that the unusual propeller spinner would only be worthwhile aerodynamically at very high speeds so it was decided to redesign Fw 190 V1. A normal NACA engine cowling was now fitted. Redesigned in this way and with the new registration FO + LY, Fw 190 V1 flew for the first time on 25 January 1940. Both the aircraft were still using the BMW 139, but there was no doubt that the Fw 190 would get a new engine.

In June 1939 BMW took over Brandenburgische Motorenwerke and negotiated a joint development agreement. One of the results of this agreement was that from 30 September 1939 all the current engine developments were terminated including the work on the BMW 139. BMW now offered the 14-cylinder double-row BMW 801 radial engine. A team under Dipl.Ing. Duckstein had been designing this engine from October 1938. In April 1939 the first 801 test engine was being run on the test bench. Although the development was still incomplete it was released in December 1939 for series production as the engine was needed for the Fw 190. Production of the BMW 801 A then began in the middle of 1940. The implications of the series production of an under-developed engine was to become clearly apparent in the further development of the Fw 190 during the coming months.

Whereas the Fw 190 V1 was still unarmed, the V2 had two synchronised MG 17s and two MG 131s in the wing roots and it was equipped with a Revi C/12C gunsight and an FuG VII radio. The dimensions of the V1 and V2 prototypes were the same: wingspan 9.515m, length 8.85m, wing area 14.9sq. m. The all-up flying weights were:

FW 190 V1: 3000kg
FW 190 V2: 3125kg.

These two aircraft (with works production numbers 01 and 02) were followed by V3 (works no. 03) and V4 (works no. 04) as flying testbeds for the first BMW 801 engines. The Fw 190 V3 was designed for the installation of a BMW 801A (clockwise running) and the V4 was to receive a BMW 801B (anti-clockwise). There is no proof as to whether these engines were ever installed. It would appear that the V3 was later cannibalised for parts to repair other test aircraft. The FW 190 V4 was used for strength and fatigue testing.

Chief Test pilot Sander in the Fw 190 cockpit

Fw 190 V1, D-OPZE in Rechlin, July 1939. From left
to right; General ingenieur Lucht, Ernst Udet,
Dipl.-Ing. Francke

Official
inspection of
Fw 190 V1: from
left to right: Ing.
Bader, Fritsche,
Francke (from
the Rechlin test
centre), Udet
and Lucht

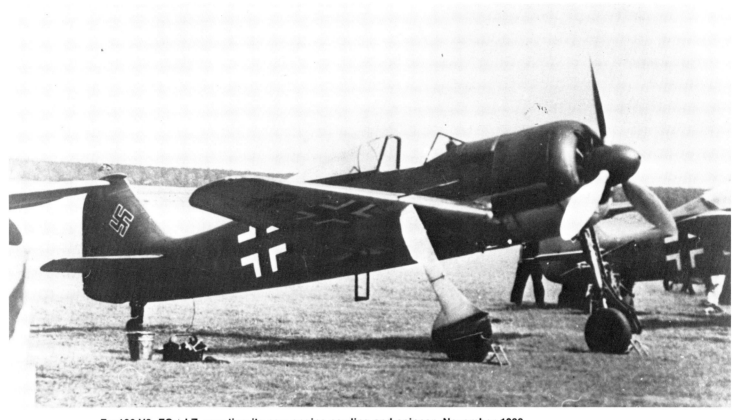

Fw 190 V2, FO + LZ, sporting its new engine cowling and spinner, November 1939

Fw 190 V1 with revised registration, FO + LY, and new engine cowling

Fw 190 V3 was the first Fw 190 to be powered by the BMW 801

BMW 139 engine showing the cooling fan

2. From Prototype to Pre-Production Run

Logically the V5 should have followed the Fw 190 V4. This, however, was to be built in two versions, the V5k (*klein* = small) with a wingspan of 9.5m, and the V5g (*groß* = big) with a wingspan of 10.383m. The length of both versions was 8.798m. The V5 was only ever built as the V5k, being powered by a BMW 801 from the C-O pre-production series. Its armament consisted only of two synchronised MG 17s and its radio equipment was the improved Funkgerät FuG VIIa. There were also a V6 and V7 but these were part of the pre-production series A-O which carried works nos. 0006 to 0045. Aircraft with nos. 0006 to 0014 had the small wing of 9.5m span, the remainder had the V5g big wing. V6 was works no. 0006, but V7 carried the number 0001 as it was the prototype for the A-1 series. It was largely similar to the V5 but had a production series BMW 801C-1 and FuG VII and FuG 125. V8 and V9 were also prototypes for the Fw 190A-1 series.

Most of the Fw 190 A-O (pre-production series) were later converted and served as prototypes for other series. Originally it was the intention at Focke-Wulf to continue with the designation A plus a number and to include heavy fighters, fighter bombers and ground attack aircraft in this A series. Developments in the war, however, showed that the Fw 190 could be used for various special purposes when suitably adapted. Focke-Wulf developed modification kits (*Umrüstsätze*) which could only be fitted in the factory or if absolutely necessary by contractors' working parties in the field. These were different from the field modifi-

cation kits (*Rüstsätze*) which were complete add-on assemblies which could easily be fitted in the field. These and parts for front-line repairs were stored at Luftzeugamt Küpper (near Sagan in Schlesien) and were delivered via the air depots to the equipment allocation points (*Geräteausgabestellen* – GASt) of the units.

The BMW 801 was far from being ready for production installation and continually caused problems but test flying of the two versions, with the small and the big wing, continued at a frenetic pace. Comparison flying between the two versions of aircraft showed that the short span aircraft was faster but that the big wing V5g version had better handling characteristics. Kurt Tank himself joined Flugkapitän Stein and Dipl.Ing. Mehlhorn for the test flying. He established that the big wing V5g version could climb so well that it could be climbed vertically. All three pilots took off to try this, Dipl.Ing. Mehlhorn doing the best in the these tests, managing to climb his Fw 190 A-O vertically to 6,215 ft!

At this stage the Technisches Amt wanted to have the Fw 190 tested by experienced battle-hardened pilots to get finally the Fw 190 (still suffering from the BMW 801 problems) ready for active service. Two officers were ordered to Rechlin. They were the Commander of 6 Staffel (squadron) of Jagdgeschwader JG 26 (fighter wing 26), Oberleutnant Otto Behrens, and the Technical Officer of JG 26, Oberleutnant Karl Borris. They had at their disposal a Focke-Wulf team of about 30 engineers and

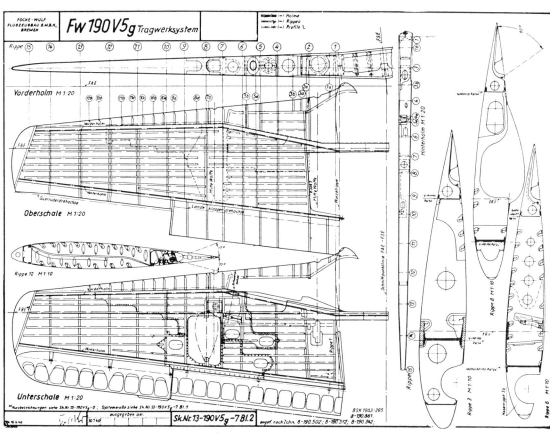

Works drawing of the Fw 190 V5g (big wing)

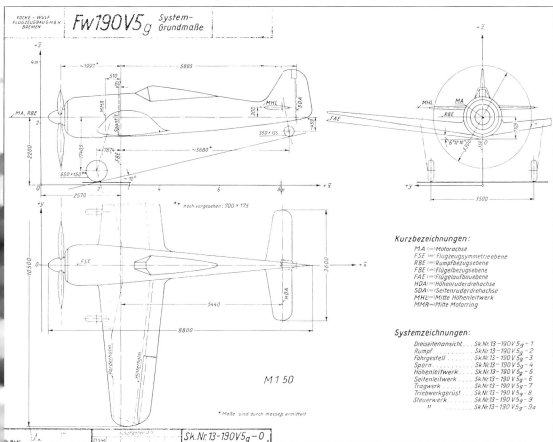

Works drawing of the Fw 190 V5g design (drawing no. 13-190- V5g-0)

17

Model of the big wing
Fw 190 V5g in the wind
tunnel

Fw 190A-0, works no. 006, prototype Fw 190 V5k (small wing)

Engine
maintenance
on the
Fw 190A-
0/U11, works
no. 0015

Undercarriage test on the same aircraft, KB + PQ

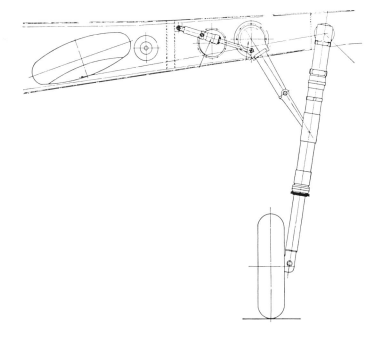

Diagram of undercarriage arrangement

mechanics. The whole FW 190 test flying team arrived at Rechlin at the end of March 1941.

The test flights themselves were made from a field which had been specially prepared for this purpose near the village of Roggentin. Behrens and Borris were enthusiastic about the Fw 190; their only complaint was the continual overheating of the BMW 801. 'Spez' Krammel, the personal friend and co-worker of Kurt Tank, acted as liaison between Focke-Wulf and the two officers. Tank himself and Dipl.Ing. Käther went to great lengths to support the team. For the men at the RLM (Reichsluftfahrtministerium) this was all taking much too long. They sent a commission to Roggentin to try to find out why the new fighter was still not ready for action. Behrens and Borris managed to convince the men from the Ministerium that the airframe itself was excellent, but that there were still problems, all of them relating to engine cooling.

Focke-Wulf Fw 190A-0, works no. 0016 (clearly showing long wing span)

Side view of previous aircraft, wing span 10.383 m

First pre-series, Fw 190A-0/U1, aircraft in Bremen. From the nearest: works nos. 0023, 0015, 0024 and 006

Oberleutnant Karl Borris, Technical Officer of JG 26, who together with Oberleutnant Behrens, 6/JG 26, did the bulk of the work in making the FW 190 ready for production

It is no exaggeration to say that without the work of Behrens and Borris the Fw 190 would never have been ready for action. It was only the addition of a cooling fan which overcame the worst of the difficulties. By the middle of 1942 it was at last possible to think in terms of a BMW 801 that was ready for production. Previously, before the cooling fan had been added, the engine had been damaged beyond repair through overheating after just twenty hours operation. As soon as the improved versions of the BMW 801 were available the Fw 190A-0 aircraft were modified as follows: Fw 190 V6 became the Fw 190A-0/U1, armed with two MG 17 over the engine and two more in the wing roots. Fw 190A-0 works nos. 0008, 0010, 0012 and 0013 had MG 131s in the wings instead of MG 17s and were designated Fw 190 A-0/U2. FW 190 A-0/U3 had modified radio equipment (works no. 0021) and was crashed in its role as V8 test aircraft on 1 October 1941. Fw 190A-0/U4 (works nos. 0022 and 0023) were fitted with under-wing stores carriers which could either take two SC 250 bombs of two 300 litre fuel tanks. Experimentally Fw 190 works nos. 0022 was fitted with an ejector seat, and 0023 was fitted with the new FuG 16Z radio equipment. The following modifications were made but seem only to have affected individual aircraft: Fw 190A-0/U5 was simi-

Fw 190A-0/U1, works no. 0022, fighter bomber trials with two SC 50 bombs under each wing and four SC 50s slung under the fuselage

Fw 190A-0/U2 with two MG17s over the engine

Fw 190A-0/U4, works no. 0022, with ETC 250 stores carrier under the fuselage and SC 250 bomb

Fw 190A-0/U4, works no. 0022, was tested with the ETC under the fuselage, here with 300 litre drop tank

Fw 190A-0/U4, works no. 0022, was fitted with the first ejector seat, here being tested with a dummy pilot

lar to A-0/U4 but had two Mg 17s, two MG 151s, and two MG/FFs. Fw 190A-0/U10 had the improved BMW 801 C-1 engine and improved MG/FF cannon. A-0/U11 had its armament changed to four Mg 17s and two MG/FFs. A-0/U12 and /U13 were similar to U11 but were fitted with the new BMW 801 C-2 engine.

3. The First Series and the Start of Active Service

The first series was the Fw 190A-1, which was produced from May to October 1941; these aircraft were numbered (0110) 001 to 102. They were armed with two MG 17s above the engine, two more in the wing roots and two MG/FFs in the outer wings. They were powered by the improved BMW 801C-1 – but this was still not without its problems.

From the start the Fw 190A-1 had been intended for use also as a fighter bomber. A kit was available (assembly 861) for adding a stores carrier (ETC 501) under the fuselage. This could either carry a 300 litre fuel tank or bombs up to 500kg. When the Fw 190 was used as a fighter bomber the inner undercarriage fairings were removed.

The first unit to be equipped with the Fw 190A-1 was II Gruppe of JG 26, which in August 1941 was at Le Bourget near Paris. Returning from Roggentin Karl Borris took over its 8 Staffel in November.

There was no way of preventing members of the French Resistance from becoming aware of the arrival of the new German fighter and dutifully informing the British. In so doing they made a mistake which was to have serious repercussions. Because of a superficial resemblance they assumed that the Germans had put the captured French Curtiss H-75 into service – which would have been no match for the British Spitfire. The British, however, were soon to notice the error. In comparison flying and mock dogfights between the Fw-190 and captured fighters Behrens and Borris had already established that the Fw 190 was superior to the Spitfire and the Hurricane in manoeuvrability and also had a superior rate of climb up to 24,600 ft.

On 27 September 1941 the fighters of II/JG 26 met British fighters for the first time. This was just a trial run with two or three machines. The Fw 190A-1 was only finally put into service with II/JG 26 in November 1941. The Commodore (Wing Commander) of JG 26, Oberstleutnant Galland had himself tested the first Fw 190 to arrive and was very satisfied with its flying characteristics, but immediately commented on the difficulties with the engine. Shortly afterwards four Fw 190A-1s met a considerably larger number of Spitfires at 12,800 ft above Gravelines. Although the Spitfires were numerically superior, the Fw 190s succeeded in shooting down three of them.

The German Secret Service reported soon afterwards that the début of the Fw 190 had made a considerable impression in Britain. Back in JG 26, however, there was less enthusiasm for the new aircraft. The man responsible for the operation of the aircraft, Fliegerstabsingenieur Battmer, wrote in a report that the Fw 190 was a catastrophe initially. Almost every flight led to engine problems. It often happened that take-off had to be abandoned because even whilst running-up the engine prior to take-off things started to go wrong. The Fw 190 manufacturers, Focke-Wulf, declared that the engine was useless, whereas BMW for their part claimed that Focke-Wulf had not provided adequate cooling for the engine. The overheating of the engine was so

The first Fw 190A-1/U1s on the tarmac at Bremen on 10 December 1942.

Installation of the BMW 801C-1 in an Fw 190A-1

extreme that the MG 17 ammunition above the engine often exploded.

It was Oberleutnant Behrens who finally succeeded in making both firms accept the modifications which were necessary (in the end there were about fifty!) to control the overheating of the BMW 801. The first engagements had already shown that the

26

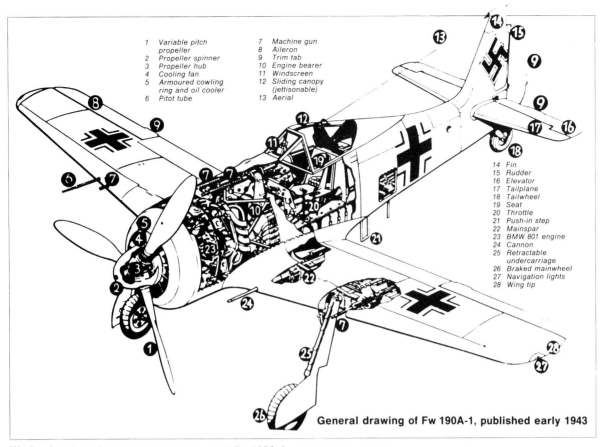

1 Variable pitch propeller
2 Propeller spinner
3 Propeller hub
4 Cooling fan
5 Armoured cowling ring and oil cooler
6 Pitot tube
7 Machine gun
8 Aileron
9 Trim tab
10 Engine bearer
11 Windscreen
12 Sliding canopy (jettisonable)
13 Aerial
14 Fin
15 Rudder
16 Elevator
17 Tailplane
18 Tailwheel
19 Seat
20 Throttle
21 Push-in step
22 Mainspar
23 BMW 801 engine
24 Cannon
25 Retractable undercarriage
26 Braked mainwheel
27 Navigation lights
28 Wing tip

General drawing of Fw 190A-1, published early 1943

Works drawing of armament arrangement Fw 190A-1

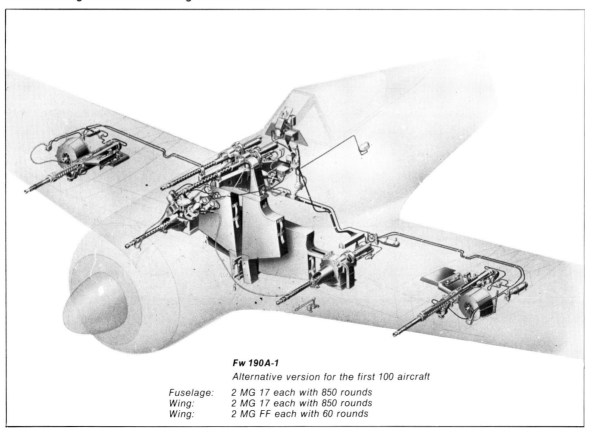

Fw 190A-1

Alternative version for the first 100 aircraft

Fuselage: 2 MG 17 each with 850 rounds
Wing: 2 MG 17 each with 850 rounds
Wing: 2 MG FF each with 60 rounds

Fw 190A-8 cockpit arrangement

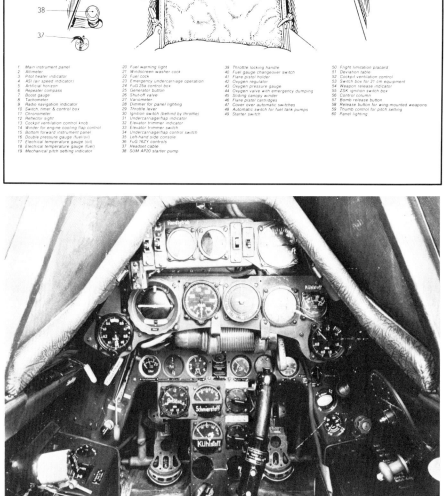

1	Main instrument panel	20	Fuel warning light
2	Altimeter	21	Windscreen washer cock
3	Pitot heater indicator	22	Fuel cock
4	ASI (air speed indicator)	23	Emergency undercarriage operation
5	Artificial horizon	24	FuG 25a control box
6	Repeater compass	25	Generator button
7	Boost gauge	26	Shut-off valve
8	Tachometer	27	Variometer
9	Radio navigation indicator	28	Dimmer for panel lighting
10	Switch, timer & control box	29	Throttle lever
11	Chronometer	30	Ignition switch (behind by throttle)
12	Reflector sight	31	Undercarriage/flap indicator
13	Cockpit ventilation control knob	32	Elevator trimmer indicator
14	Winder for engine cooling flap control	33	Elevator trimmer switch
15	Bottom forward instrument panel	34	Undercarriage/flap control switch
16	Double pressure gauge (fuel/oil)	35	Left-hand side console
17	Electrical temperature gauge (oil)	36	FuG 16ZY controls
18	Electrical temperature gauge (fuel)	37	Headset cable
19	Mechanical pitch setting indicator	38	SUM AP20 starter pump

39	Throttle locking handle	50	Flight limitation placard
40	Fuel gauge changeover switch	51	Deviation table
41	Flare pistol holder	52	Cockpit ventilation control
42	Oxygen regulator	53	Switch box for 21 cm equipment
43	Oxygen pressure gauge	54	Weapon release indicator
44	Oxygen valve with emergency dumping	55	ZSK ignition switch box
45	Sliding canopy winder	56	Control column
46	Flare pistol cartridges	57	Bomb release button
47	Cover over automatic switches	58	Release button for wing-mounted weapons
48	Automatic switch for fuel tank pumps	59	Thumb control for pitch setting
49	Starter switch	60	Panel lighting

Fw 190 instrument panel

28

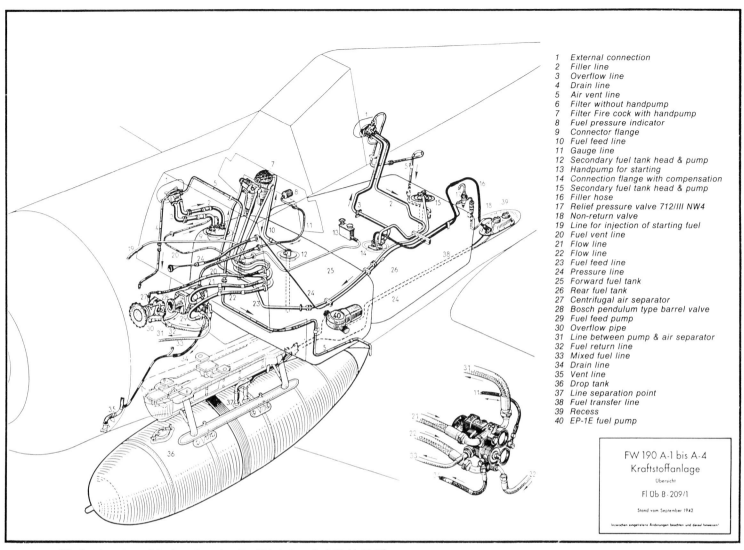

1 External connection
2 Filler line
3 Overflow line
4 Drain line
5 Air vent line
6 Filter without handpump
7 Filter Fire cock with handpump
8 Fuel pressure indicator
9 Connector flange
10 Fuel feed line
11 Gauge line
12 Secondary fuel tank head & pump
13 Handpump for starting
14 Connection flange with compensation
15 Secondary fuel tank head & pump
16 Filler hose
17 Relief pressure valve 712/III NW4
18 Non-return valve
19 Line for injection of starting fuel
20 Fuel vent line
21 Flow line
22 Flow line
23 Fuel feed line
24 Pressure line
25 Forward fuel tank
26 Rear fuel tank
27 Centrifugal air separator
28 Bosch pendulum type barrel valve
29 Fuel feed pump
30 Overflow pipe
31 Line between pump & air separator
32 Fuel return line
33 Mixed fuel line
34 Drain line
35 Vent line
36 Drop tank
37 Line separation point
38 Fuel transfer line
39 Recess
40 EP-1E fuel pump

FW 190 A-1 bis A-4
Kraftstoffanlage
Übersicht
Fl Üb 8·209/1
Stand vom September 1942
Inzwischen eingetretene Änderungen beachten und darauf hinweisen!

Works drawing of fuel system for Fw 190 A-1 to A-4 (3.11.1941)

Fw 190A-1 was under-weaponed, so a second prototype for a new A-2 version was created, the Fw 190 V14, works no. (0120)201. Whereas the A-1 had MG 17s in the wing roots, these had MG 151s, and the BMW 801C-1 was replaced by the improved BMW 801C-2. A total of 425 A-2 version aircraft were built between August 1941 and July 1942, some of them as Fw 190A-2/U1s, in which the FuG VII and FuG 25 radio equipment had been extended by the install-ation of PKS direction finding equipment.

Another difference between the A-1 and A-2 was the undercarriage indicator which con-sisted of two rods which projected from the upper surface of the leading edge of the wing when the undercarriage was extended. The undercarriage indicator was disconti-nued, however, from the next series onwards.

The modifications to the engine and the airframe which were meant to put an end to the Fw 190 engine problems were carried out on Fw 190A-0 works nos. 0014, 0025 and

0028. The BMW 801C-2 engine with its final modifications was installed in them; its performance had been increased from 1560 to 1770 PS. An Fw 190A-2 (works no. 315) was experimentally fitted with an ETC 501 under the fuselage which could either carry a 300 litre fuel tank or an SC 250 bomb. As the BMW 801D-2 was an airworthy engine and available, a large proportion of the Fw 190A-2s were changed to this engine without changing their type designation. At the same time the following Bf 109 units were changed to Fw 190As: II, III and IV Gruppe of JG 1, I, II and III Gruppe of JG 2, and I, II and III Gruppe of JG 26. All these formations were in the west.

In the summer of 1942 some of the Fw 190A-2s were modified to A-2/U3 which was better armoured through the installation of thicker sheet-steel panels. The Fw 190A-0s, (works nos. 0014, 0025 and 0028) can be regarded as prototypes of the new A3 series of which 580 were built between February and August 1942. The main difference to the previous series were the *Kiemenspalten* gills (air exit flaps) which had become necessary through engine modifications. In addition to the units already mentioned, the Fw 190 was now issued also to JG 51, Schlachtgeschwader (ground attack squadrons) 1 and 2 and 9(H)/LG 2 (reconnaissance). Fw 190A-3/U3 (works no. 300) was thoroughly tested for use by ground attack squadrons in the wind tunnel at Chalais-Meudon where it was fitted with various carriers and attachment devices. The external identification feature of the Fw 190A-3 was the bulge modification on the side of the engine cowling. Whereas on aircraft up to the A-2 it was a symmetrical streamlined shape, the end of the bulge now flowed upwards at the back.

Although the squadrons of both ground attack wings had changed to the Fw 190A from late August 1942, it was only on 17 December 1942 that Schlachtgeschwader (SG) 1 was ordered to divide into three Staffel of Fw 190s and an anti-tank squadron of Henschel Hs 129s. 5/SG 1 decamped in December 1942 to North Africa as 8(Pz)/SG 2. At the same time SG 2 were ordered to do the same. The first two groups of SG 2 were equipped with only the Fw 190 from the beginning of Spring 1943.

A whole series of Fw 190 A-3s were tested for serviceability in various respects after modification. Fw 190A-3/U1, PG + GY, works no. 130270 was to become a 'Grosser Jabo' (big fighter bomber). A-3/U2, works no. 130386, was equipped experimentally with RZ 65 rockets, spin stabilised with a range of about 330 yards; these were manufactured by Rheinmetall-Borsig and used as an anti-tank grenade for attacking ground targets. They were particularly effective in attacks on railway locomotives. Fw 190A-3/U3, works no. (0130)511, was fitted with tropical filters for operation in North Africa. The Fw 190A-3/U4 was a fighter reconnaissance aircraft with Rb 50/30 and Rb 75/30 series topographical cameras. Twelve normal A-3 aircraft were converted and went to 9(H)/LG 2. This unit was based in Jüterborg-Damm, which served as a test base for single-seater reconnaissance aircraft, and it later became a replacement group for these units. Three Fw 190A-3/U7s (works nos. 526, 530 and 531) were intended as light high altitude fighters. They had the following external identification features: external air intakes, adjustable cooling air flaps and armament reduced to two MG 151s in the

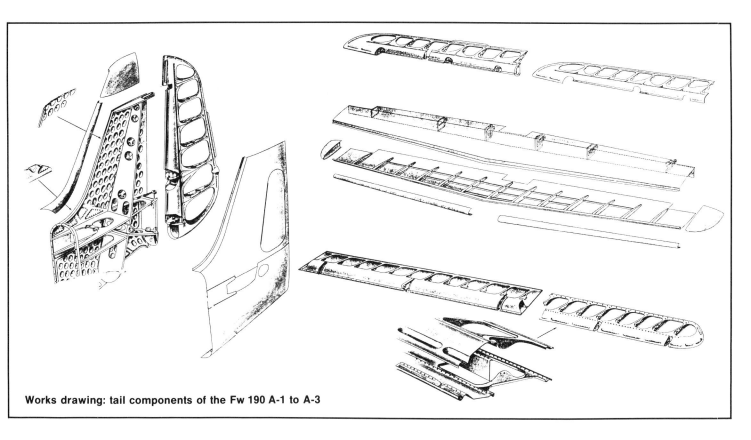

Works drawing: tail components of the Fw 190 A-1 to A-3

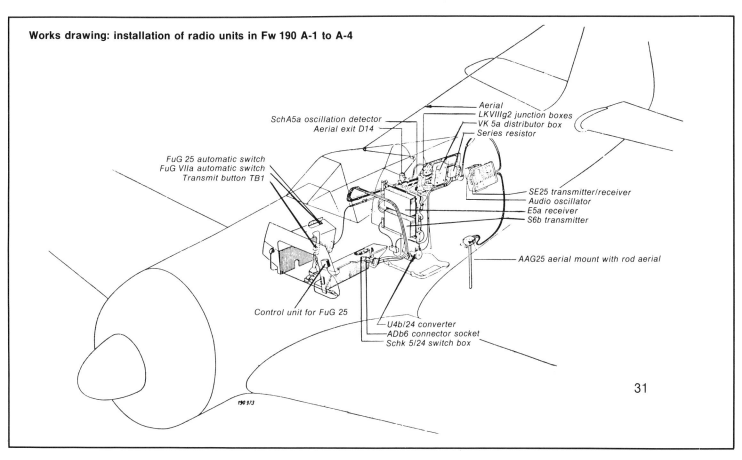

Works drawing: installation of radio units in Fw 190 A-1 to A-4

Aerial
LKVIIIg2 junction boxes
SchA5a oscillation detector
VK 5a distributor box
Aerial exit D14
Series resistor

FuG 25 automatic switch
FuG VIIa automatic switch
Transmit button TB1

SE25 transmitter/receiver
Audio oscillator
E5a receiver
S6b transmitter

AAG25 aerial mount with rod aerial

Control unit for FuG 25

U4b/24 converter
ADb6 connector socket
Schk 5/24 switch box

190 973

31

Fw 190 A-1 of
II/JG 26, September
1941 in France

Fw 190 A-1 belonging to 8/JG 2 (works no. 0033)

Fw 190A-1 on naval protection duties in the Channel

Major Adolf Galland, Kommodore of JG 26 (third from left), Fw 190A-1 in the background

Fw 190A-2. The indicator rods confirming that the undercarriage is lowered are visible above the wing

Works drawing of Fw 190 A-1 to A-4

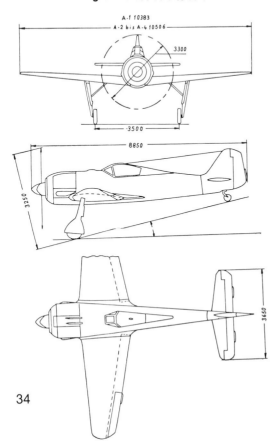

A-1 10383
A-2 bis A-4 10506
3300
3500
8850
3250
3650

wing roots. Whether these aircraft were ever used operationally is not known.

From October 1942 to March 1943 there was a special production programme running parallel to normal production. This production programme, known as 'Hamburg', was an export order of 72 Fw 190Aa-3s for Turkey. This type was basically the same as the Fw 190A-1/U1. Because the British also supplied a number of Spitfires to Turkey at the same time it means that the otherwise mutually hostile aircraft were flying peacefully side by side.

Fw 190A-2, works no. 120228, of III/JG 2

Fw 190A-2 at Bordeaux-Merignac; in the background Do 217E of KG 40

Fw 190A-2, works no.
120121, with
undercarriage bay open

Final assembly of one of
the first Fw 190A-3s at
Bremen

Test flying Fw 190A-3, works no. 130471 on 1 June 1942

The same aircraft from a different angle

Two Fw 190A-3s of JG 26 during the Battle of Britain

Fw 190A-3, BD + ? with JG 54 in Gatschina, on the northern section of the Eastern Front

Fw 190A-3 in the Chalais-Meudon wind tunnel (France)

Fw 190A-3/U1 with Focke-Wulf bomb carriers under the wing

Fw 190A-3/U2, works no. 135386, testing spin-stabilised RZ 65 rockets

Fw 190A-3/U3 with ETC 501 rack, ER 4 rack and eight SC 50 bombs in the Chalais-Meudon wind tunnel

Fw 190A-3/U3, works no. 132311, with Focke-Wulf bomb carrier

Fw 190A-3/U3, works no. 447 with ETC 501 bomb carrier

The same aircraft with ER 4 carrier adaptor for SC 50 bombs

41

Camera installation (Rb 12/7.5x9) in the Fw 190A-3/U4 short range reconnaissance aircraft

Hatch for camera access on Fw 190A-3/U4

Fw 190A-3/U4 with EK 16 Robot camera in the wing

Light high altitude fighter Fw 190A-3/U7, works no.137528

Fw 190Aa-3 export version for Turkey

4. The Third, Fourth and Fifth Series

Initially the main factory at Bremen was able to cope with the required production but by 1942 Focke-Wulf had to bring in several other firms to meet the requirements of the RLM. The main firms building aircraft under licence were AGO-Werke at Oschersleben and Fieseler-Flugzeugwerke at Kassel-Waldau. As the required production figures went on increasing the Focke-Wulf factories at Marienburg and Tutow and other factories at Gdingen (Gotenhafen), Sorau, Cottbus, Halberstadt, Neubrandenburg, Schwerin, Wismar, Einswarden and Eschwege were enlisted. In 1941 just 226 Fw 190s had been built but by 1942 production had already risen to 1918, comprising 1850 fighters and 68 ground attack aircraft.

The British had realised that Bremen was breeding a very dangerous opponent. British long-distance reconnaissance aircraft had very little difficulty in taking crystal clear photographs of the factories. During the night of 12 March 1941 the first attack by British Bomber Command took place. 54 Vickers Wellingtons bombed the Focke-Wulf factory whilst 32 Bristol Blenheims bombed the town. 21 Wellingtons missed their target. The remaining 33 dropped 132 high explosive bombs and 840 incendiary bombs on the factory. The design office was particularly badly damaged and numerous Fw 190 plans and drawings went up in flames.

Fw 190s were regularly engaged in dogfights along the channel coast in which both JG 2 and JG 26 were involved, but the Fw 190 really had its baptism of fire on 12 February 1942 in operation 'Cerberus-Donnerkeil' in which two battleships, *Scharnhorst* and *Gneisenau,* and also the heavy cruiser *Prinz Eugen*, braved their way up the English Channel.

Shortly before that, Oberstleutnant Galland had succeeded Oberst Werner Mölders as Inspekteur der Jagdflieger, (Inspector General, Fighters), Mölders having been killed on 22 November 1941. Galland was now responsible for air protection for this breakthrough by the German Navy.

Galland took control of the situation from a command post on land but there was a liaison headquarters on board the *Scharnhorst,* headed by Oberst Ibel, attached to which there were also two fighter control officers and Oberst Elle with several radio operators as communications officers. Galland had divided the area into five operational areas: Ia (Le Havre-Cherbourg), Ib (Le Havre), I (Abbeville-Calais), II (The Rhine Estuary to the Schelde Estuary) and III (Jever-Wilhelmshaven). JG 2 in Caen, ready for action with 90 Fw 190s, were to protect area Ia, area Ib was to be protected by the Jagdschule (fighter training unit) in Paris with twelve Bf 109Fs based at Le Touquet, area I was the responsiblity of JG 26 with 90 Fw 190s based at Le Touquet and JG 1 at Jever was responsible for the rest, with 60 Fw 190s. The fighter aircraft succeeded in warding off all attacks on the ships and the only damage to the ships was caused by mines. Despite the mine damage, all the ships succeeded in reaching German ports.

Production of the next series, the Fw 190A-4, was started parallel to the

One of the first Fw 190A-4s

Fw 190A-4 belonging to I/JG 3

Fw 190A-4 belonging to I/JG 1 in Holland, 1943

Crash landing at Arnhem 1942. An Fw 190A-4 belonging to IV/JG 1

Fw 190A-4 flown by Hauptmann Priller, Commander of III/JG 26

production of the Fw 190A-3. It began in June 1942 and continued until January 1943 during which time a total of 906 Fw 190A-4s were produced. The main external characteristics which differentiate the A-4 from all previous series were the modified fin and the short FuG 16 aerial mast. In 1942 1/JG 54 was the first unit on the Eastern Front to receive Fw 190As to replace the Bf 109. This changeover began on 25 November 1942.

During 1942 the Fw 190A was flown, in various versions, by Jagdgeschwader 1, 2, 5, 11, 26, 51, 54, 300, Schnellkampfgeschwader (SKG) 10 (rapid response), Schlachtgeschwader 1 and 2 (ground attack), Fernaufklärungsgruppe 123 (long-range reconnaissance) and Nahaufklärungsgruppe 13 (short-range reconnaissance).

The Fw 190A-4 was very similar to the A-3 but its armament consisted of two MG 17s, two MG 151/20s and two MG/FFs. The ETC 501 stores carrier could easily be added, and the radio equipment consisted of the FuG 16Z and the FuG 25. Numerous variants of the Fw 190A-4 were produced.

The first aircraft in the A-4 series, works no. (0140)561, was used as the prototype for the series and identified as Fw 190 V24. Originally it had the BMW 801C-1 engine but was soon fitted with the BMW 801C-2 instead and thereafter these aircraft were designated Fw 190A-4/U1. When used as a fighter bomber the MG/FFs in the wing and sometimes also the synchronised MG 17s were removed and it flew with just two MG 151/20s and 500kg bombs. These aircraft were flown by Schlachtkampfgeschwader SKG 10 amongst others. For night

47

Oberfeldwebel Adolf
Glunz, II/JG 26,
jumping from the
cockpit of his
Fw 190A-4 after
landing

Dust filter
arrangement on the
tropicalised
Fw 190A-4

operations landing lights were fitted under
the port wing.

One variant, known as the A-4/U3, had
reinforced armour-plating for ground attack.
Thirty were built and these were the forerun-
ners of the F-1 series. All the A-4/U3s were
redesignated Fw 190F-1 in April 1943. Some
of the machines were fitted with tropical
filters for operations in North Africa. An
ETC 501 stores carrier was installed under
the fuselage.

The A-4/U4 was a fighter reconnaissance
aircraft similar to the A-3/U4. It too could be
identified by the camera bulge under the
fuselage but it differed from the A-3/U4 in its
small aerial mast on the fin. Only a small
number of A-4/U1 aircraft were built and
they were used by 5(F)/123 and NaGr 13
(short-range reconnaissance). In these
aircraft the FuG VII was replaced by the

FuG 17. In addition they had a Robot camera
(a 35mm camera with fixed-focus lens
produced by the firm of Robot) in the leading

Fw 190A-4/U3, prototype for the ground attack F-1 version, works no. 140619, with ETC 501, ER 4 carrier adaptor and four SC 50s

Fw 190A-4/U3 with ETC 501 and two SC 100 bombs under the wings

Training of short-range reconnaissance pilots on an Fw 190A-4/U4 at Reinsdorf, August 1943. The pilot is Oberleutnant Reschke

edge of the port wing. The A-4/U8 was a long-range fighter bomber, similar to the A-4/U1 and armed with just two MG 151/20s in the wing roots, an ETC 501 carrier under the fuselage for 500kg bombs and Junkers stores carriers under the wings for two 300 litre fuel tanks. There were semi-circular cut-outs in the landing flaps to prevent them touching the fuel tanks. Two prototypes were built, works nos. (0140) 669 and 670, and in April 1943 they were redesignated Fw 190G-1.

The Fw 190A-4/R1 was a normal A-4/U1 but was equipped with the FuG 16Z-E for the so-called 'Y System' and so could be

Fw 190A-4/U4 with 1(F)/123 in Italy 1943

Fw 190A-4/U8 extended-range fighter bomber, precursor of the G series (Jaborei)

Fw 190A-4/U8 with 300 litre tank and Junkers carrier

recognised by the circular frame aerial under the fuselage. Only unit and formation leaders flew these aircraft. At the instigation of General Kammhuber the FuG 16Z-E was developed from the FuG 16Z so that it could send and transmit simultaneously. A ground station, *Wotan III*, was equipped with range finder equipment with the S 16B transmitter and the E 16E receiver and a VHF direction finder which had been modified to the FuG 16 frequency and was known as 'Heinrich'. The Y system used a ground transmitter which transmitted a range-finding tone for five seconds every twenty seconds. This was received by the lead aircraft (Fw 190 A-4/R1) and transmitted back on a lower frequency. The signal was received by the range-finding equipment to establish the distance, and by the VHF direction finder to confirm the direction. The other aircraft

Fw 190A-4/U8, works no. 140128, heavy fighter bomber with ETC 501 and SB 1000 bomb. Note that the lower fin has had to be removed from the tail of the bomb to prevent contact with the ground

Fw 190A-4/R1 fighter bomber of the I/JG 54 (Eastern Front)

The same type with SC 250 bomb, in the west

Launching tube for W.Gr.21 slung under the wing of the Fw 190A-4/R6

Fw 190A-4/R6 *Pulkzerstörer* **(bomber formation destroyer) with 21cm mortars (W.Gr.21)**

used the same frequency as the ground station so that they could communicate with the lead aircraft and also amongst themselves. The location of the fighters was transmitted to fighter control bases where the location of the enemy aircraft had also been received. In this way the fighter formation could be guided towards the enemy.

From the summer of 1943 onwards there were a few so-called Fw 190A-4/R6 *Pulkzerstörer* (formation destroyers). These were equipped with WGr 21 rocket launchers under the wings. They had their greatest success on 14 October 1943 when the 8th USAAF attacked the VKF and FAG ballbearing factories at Schweinfurt with 228 Boeing B-17s. The Fw 190A-4/R6s of Jagdgeschwader 1 and 26 were able to fire their rockets from outside the range of the B-17 gunners. Altogether 62 bombers were shot down and 17 more crashed over England, but many Germany fighters were also lost. The Americans claimed at the time that 186 were lost but in fact the figure was only 50. On 23 June 1942 the British finally received what they had been trying to get – and it was delivered free of charge to their very door:

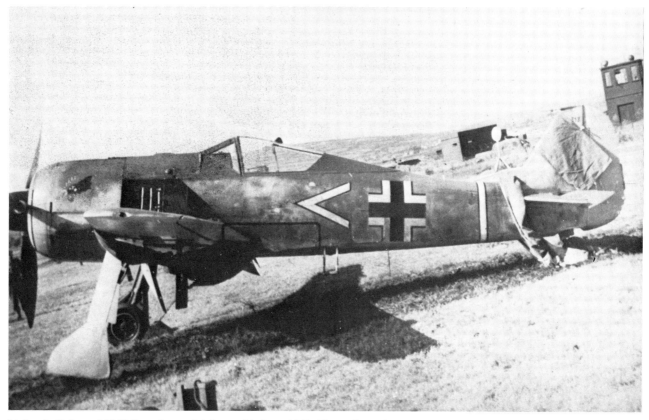

Lt Armin Faber of 7/JG 2 made a mistake on 23 June 1942. Through navigational error he landed his Fw 190A-3, works no. 130313, at RAF Pembrey. This aircraft was given MP 499 as its British identification number and tested extensively

an undamaged ready-to-fly Fw 190. Leutnant Faber of II/JG 2 lost his way after being engaged in battle over England and landed at Pembrey. His aircraft was Fw 190A-3, works no. (0130) 313. He was overpowered before he could set fire to his aircraft. The aircraft was shortly test flown by RAF personnel.

On 17 July a party of Americans including Colonel Grainger, Lieutenant Colonel Sparkes, Major Turner, Major Hitchcock and Major Stalling were invited to witness a dogfight between Faber's Fw 190 and a Spitfire IX. Five days later further dogfights between the Fw 190, a Spitfire IX, a Spitfire XII and a Hawker Typhoon were simulated at the Air Fighting Development Unit, Duxford.

On 19 August 1942 the Allies landed at Dieppe and deployed 56 squadrons of the Royal Air Force. The Germans had virtually only Jagdgeschwader 2 and 26 with which to oppose them, but despite these odds the Germans lost only 48 fighters whereas the British and Canadians lost 106 aircraft. Most of the Fw 190s had been destroyed or badly damaged but what was even worse was that the air depot at Welveghem had been badly hit and the reserve aircraft badly damaged. All the 20mm ammunition had been destroyed, and it was not until the next day that fresh ammunition could be brought in by Ju 52 in an airlift between Fürstenwalde and Beauvais.

The first contact between an Fw 190 and an American Mustang fighter took place on 27 July. Although this was the earlier

Supermarine Spitfire F. MkIX, as used for comparison flying with the captured Fw 190

version of the Mustang fitted with the Allison V-1710 engine, the Fw 190A-3 could not catch up with the Mustang which it pursued from Dieppe to Eastbourne. A second Mustang, however was shot down.

On 30 August 1942 an Fw 190 shot the tail off an RAF Lockheed Lightning (AE 979) and it crashed, though the British pilot parachuted to safety. On 6 December 1942 there was a real bloodbath when Fw 190s attacked 47 Lockheed Venturas (a development of the Hudson) and 36 Douglas Bostons which were on a bomb run to the Philips factories at Eindhoven. Although there was a div-

This photo of a British Hawker Typhoon confirms the similarity of its plan view with that of the Fw 190

Fw 190A-4/U8 of Schnellkampfgeschwader (rapid response) SKG 10. Like Leutnant Faber its pilot had made a navigational error and landed at West Malling in England. It was then painted in British colours, given PE 882 identification number and tested extensively by the RAF

ersionary attack on Lille by Boeing B-17s which attracted fighter attention, the Fw 190s proved effective amongst the Allied bombers. Of the 47 Venturas, nine were shot down and only one escaped undamaged; of the 36 Bostons five were shot down and 13 badly damaged.

It became apparent on the same day, however, that one British type was superior to the Fw 190. Ten Mosquito bombers met a formation of Fw 190s and were forced to break off their bombing attack. All of them escaped from the Fw 190s although one Fw 190 only gave up the chase when over Flushing (near Great Yarmouth) in England.

The British had a serious problem. They had set high hopes on the new Hawker Typhoon which was to make up for the weakness of the Spitfire V and Hawker Hurricane II. The problem was that in the air the Typhoon so closely resembled the Fw 190 that it was being shot down by British fighters and British flak. The problem was so serious that withdrawing the Typhoon from the front was seriously considered. It was not until November 1942 when foot wide black and white stripes were painted on the underside of the fuselage that a solution was

Yet another navigational error. On the 20 May 1943 Unteroffizier Heinz Ehrhardt of 1/SKG 10 accidentally landed his Fw 190A-4/U8, works no. 155843, at RAF Manston in England. The auxiliary tanks on the Ju 87 carriers have been removed

found to the problem.

The recently-introduced Fw 190 also proved effective on the Eastern Front, Leutnant Schack and Leutnant Dittmann of Jagdgeschwader 51 being particularly successful. On 23 February 1943 I and II/JG 51 shot down 46 Russian aircraft. Schack and his comrade Jennewein, the Olympic skiing champion, each shot down five Russian aircraft.

JG 54, under the command of Oberstleutnant (Wing Commander) Trautloft, was in the Leningrad area at the end of 1942. From 25 November 1942 the squadrons were sent

one by one to Heiligenbeil, west of Königsberg in East Prussia, for modification of their aircraft into Fw 190A-4s. From his very first flights in the new aircraft it became clear to Trautloft that: 'Compared with the Me 109 the Fw 190 as a fighting machine was considerably more robust, and with its heavier armament was more suitable for fighting low-flying ground attack aircraft (Ilyushin IL-2). The Fw 190 was less susceptible to bullet damage than the Me 109 and for this reason it was preferred by pilots for ground attack which was often necessary in our sector in the northern part of the Eastern

Front. But the Me 109 was preferred for fighter-to-fighter confrontation especially at great altitude.'

This view was expressed in a letter from Trautloft to the author. In his last sentence Trautloft mentions the weakness of the Fw 190A, in that the BMW 801 was an excellent engine up to a height of about 25,000 ft but above that height its performance fell off. This was to remain the case until the end of the war, which explains why the Fw 190 A and all versions equipped with the BMW 801 were used almost exclusively as ground attack aircraft and fighter bombers.

In the west, the head Chief of Luftflotte (Air Fleet) 3, Generalfeldmarschall Sperrle, ordered that in Jagdgeschwader 2 and 26, which had been at his disposal from 10 March 1942, 10 Staffel should be converted to fighter bombers. Fw 190A-4/U1s and A-4/U8s were used for this purpose, and the transition was completed in July 1942. To avoid detection by British radar the fighter bombers had to fly extremely low; they often returned to base with tree damage to their wings. Initially these fighter bomber squadrons were extremely successful.

One of the most effective raids was on 20 January 1943. In this, small unit of fighters engaged in diversionary operations over the Isle of Wight and East Kent and distracted the attention of British fighter defence, allowing large formations of Fw 190s, some of them fighter bombers, to attack London at midday. The British anti-aircraft artillery installations were taken by surprise and because the Fw 190s were flying extremely low the heavy flak could not be brought to bear on them, and the British fighters did not arrive in time. There were heavy civilian losses, a school in Catford suffering a direct hit, as did large warehouses in the Surrey Docks.

On the basis of experience with the fighter bomber squadrons a rapid response squadron was set up on 1 December 1942 consisting entirely of Fw 190A-4s. This was Schnellkampfgeschwader 10 (SKG 10), whose IV Gruppe consisted of the previous fighter bomber squadrons of JG 2 and 26. SKG 10 was based at St Andre in France.

Leutnant Faber's gift of an Fw 190A-3 at an earlier date was repeated when an A-4/U8 fell into British hands through the pilot landing on English soil at West Malling by mistake. This aircraft was painted in RAF colours, allocated number PE 882 and then subjected to an intensive test programme.

To improve the Fw 190 engine protection against gunfire, Fw 190A-4 (works no. 665) was fitted with a smaller engine cowling and was used for testing a new and stronger armoured ring protecting the engine.

Series production of the new series Fw 190A-5 began in November 1942.

5. The Fw 190 Fights to Defend its Factories

Series production continued unchecked from the A-4 to the A-5 without a break by modifying the standard A4 series aircraft. The BMW 801D-2 engine was moved forwards and additional metal cowls were added between the wing root leading edge and the engine cowling. In place of the previous air outlet slots there were adjustable air cooling gills. A larger servicing cowl was fitted on the port side of the fuselage between formers 9 and 10, and a camera, the ESK 16, was built in to the port wing tip. These aircraft were test flown by Ergänzungsjagdgruppe Süd (Fighter Replacement Group South) under the direction of Major Graf who took over command of the Ergänzungsjagdgruppe Ost (Fighter Replacement Group, East) and JG 50 after his 200th kill.

JG 50 was only set up in the summer of 1943 at Wiesbaden-Erbenheim and consisted of two reinforced squadrons. The formation had been created specially to combat American bomber formations but it was disbanded again as early as November 1943. The Fw 190A-5 in its various forms was the starting point for numerous new versions of the Fw 190.

To put an end to the confusion of various versions all series were renamed from April 1943. The letter A was retained for the fighters and light fighter bombers powered by the BMW 801. A new series B was to be a high altitude fighter powered by the BMW 801 D-2 and using GM-1 injection

Fw 190A-5, works no. 151183, BG + KC, at Forli, Italy

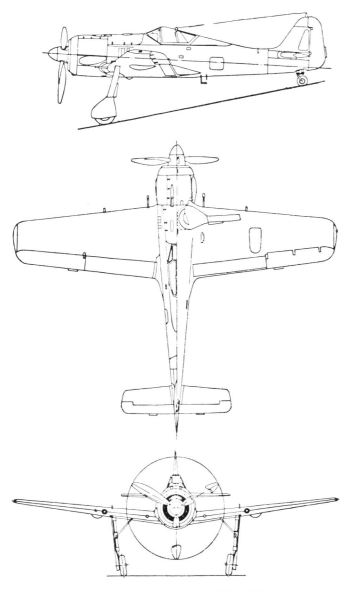

General arrangement drawing of Fw 190A-5

power boost. A series C was also to be high altitude fighters but powered by the Daimler-Benz DB 603, some of them with exhaust-driven superchargers (turbo-superchargers). The Fw 190 D was to be powered by the Jumo 213 to improve on the

Fw 190A's high altitude performance. The Fw 190E was to be a reconnaissance aircraft but was given up in favour of the U4 modified aircraft. Ground attack aircraft powered by the BMW 801 were now designated F and fighter bombers G.

In this context it is worth mentioning that in the report III/157/43 from Messerschmitt that deals with a comparison of weights between a planned Me 209 fighter and the Fw 190D, the latter is referred to as the Ta 153 with 'Fw 190D' in brackets.

The previously mentioned A-3/U1, works no. 270, can be seen as the prototype for the A-5 series in which the engine was first moved forwards. It went to Rechlin on 2 August 1943 for evaluation flying. Altogether 723 Fw 190A-5s were built. Ten machines were built with the V5k (short wing span) wing for the stress testing of aluminium alloys and these were designated Fw 190A-5k.

From the end of 1943 onwards the design of the Fw 190 wing produced some production problems because sheet aluminium was used for the wing spars. It was produced in a special rolling process which reduced the thickness of the sheet aluminium, tapering it spanwise towards the wing tips. Some of these aluminium sheets were produced in the Junkers factory at Schönebeck, and when this was damaged by bombing there was, naturally, a production bottleneck.

The Fw 190A-5/U1 was very similar to the Fw 190A-4 after it had been fitted with the BMW 801C-2 engine. The A-5/U2 version may be seen as a predecessor of the A-5/U8 version. There is evidence that at least eight aircraft were built, works nos. 711, 783, 1140, 1450, 1482 and 1513. They were used as

In 1943 Fw 190A-5/U2 was redesignated Fw 190G-2/N (Nachtjaborei) – long range night fighter bomber

Fw 190A-5/U8 was the precursor of the Fw 190G-1 series (works no. 151414)

Fw 190A-5/U8, GH + JD, was the precursor of the G-2 series

extended-range fighter bombers. Various shrouds were fitted on the exhaust of nos. 711 and 783 for night operations. The anti-dazzle shrouded exhaust arrangement finally selected was by no means satisfactory.

The Fw 190A-5/U2 had a 'Robot' camera in the port wing and a double landing light next to it. The machines were used by SKG 10. It is possible that some of these machines were also flown by the staff of JG 300. When all the Fw 190s were renamed in April 1943, as described above, these aircraft were then designated Fw 190G-2/N.

The prototypes for the F-2 series were the Fw 190A-5/U3 which were always delivered with tropical filters. They only had normal stores carriers and the usual rearward armour plating. The armament consisted of two MG 17s and two MG 151s, both with sand protection seals around the muzzle. These machines were in service with all ground

MG 121/20 installation in the wing of Fw 190A-5/U9, works no. 150812

Fw 190A-5/U11, works no. 1303 with 3 cm MK 103 cannon was the prototype of the planned Fw 190F 3/R3 anti-tank fighter series

Fw 190A-5/U12, works no. 813, BH + CC, was to become the prototype for the A-6/R1 series

attack groups from October 1943 onwards. They were particularly effective in central Italy in II/SG 4 of Air Fleet 2.

An Fw 190A-5/U4 reconnaissance aircraft, similar to the A-3/U4 and A-4/U4 predecessors, was planned but was probably never built. A further 'Jaborei' – Jagdbomber mit vergrößerter Reichweite (fighter bomber with increased range) – was the Fw 190A-5/U8. The prototypes, works nos. 813, 1286 and 1288, led to a series of about 80 aircraft which were then renamed Fw 190G-1 in April 1943. The first aircraft were still fitted with 'Weserflug' (Ju 87) stores carriers which reduced the speed of the Fw 190 to 298 mph. To overcome this Fw 190A-5/U8, GH + JD, was equipped with jettisonable Messerschmitt carriers for 300 litre drop tanks. This version was named the Fw 190G-2. The MG 17s and wing-mounted MG/FFs were no longer fitted so these aircraft simply had two MG 151s in the wing roots.

The Fw 190A-5/U9 served as a prototype (of which two were built – works nos. 812 and 816) for the later series versions A-7, A-8 and F-8. In these the MG 17s was replaced by MG 131s, there were two MG 151/20s in the wing roots and two MG/FFs in the outer wings. The ETC 501 stores carrier could take bombs up to 500kg. This version used a new wing of 10.506m span compared with the previous span of 10.383m. This wing was now fitted to all Fw 190As. The Fw 190A-5/U10, works nos. 861 and 862, differed from the A-5/U9 in that the wing-mounted MG/FFs were exchanged for MG 151/20s.

There was only ever one example of an A-5/U11 built; this was works no. 1303. This aircraft was designed as an anti-tank fighter and was to have wing-mounted MK 103s (3cm calibre) instead of MG 151s. It is doubtful whether it ever saw active service. Works no. 1303 then became the prototype for the planned A-8/R3, F-3/R3 and F-8/R3 series.

A-5/U12, works no. 813, BH + CC, was a heavy fighter armed with two MG 17s over the engine, two MG 151/20s in the wing roots and a WB 151 weapon pod under each wing, each containing two MG 151/20s. This aircraft was intended as the prototype for the A-6/R1 series. Works no. 814, BH + CD, was equipped with the so-called *Grosse Bombenelectric* (literally the 'big electric bombing system') which was intended to provide individual release of wing and fuselage bombs. But the tests were not satisfactory and consequently only 813's weapon system was maintained. Only three prototypes were produced of a 'Jaborei', the Fw 190A-5/U13, namely V42, works no. 817, BH + CG, for daytime operations, V43, works

no. 1083, GC + LA, for night operations, and V44, works no. 855, as prototype for the planned G-1 series. Aircraft works no. 1083 was tested with various anti-dazzle shields and shrouds round the exhausts, one of which, the so-called *Kohlenkasten* (coal scuttle), was fitted under the engine and in front of the ETC Stores Carrier. Aircraft numbers 817 and 1083 still had their 300 litre drop tanks attached to Messerschmitt stores carriers, whereas works no. 855 had Focke-Wulf carriers. This aircraft was also later fitted with the so-called 'Kuto nose' wing leading edge balloon cable cutter.

Fw 190 V43, works no. 1083, was the prototype for a G-3N series and was fitted with landing lights in the port wing. It was armed simply with an MG 151 in each wing root. Number 855 was to be the prototype for the planned G-4 series which was never realised, however, because the G-3 series ran on until Spring 1944.

At this time there was a requirement for a fast torpedo-carrying aircraft and this led to the construction of Fw 190A-5/U14 prototypes, works nos. 871 and 872, TD + SI, was first sent for testing to the torpedo testing station at Eckernförde in Schleswig-Holstein

Fw 190 V44, works no. 855 was also to become the prototype of the G-1 (Jaborei) long range fighter bomber series. A 300 litre drop tank is fitted under the wing

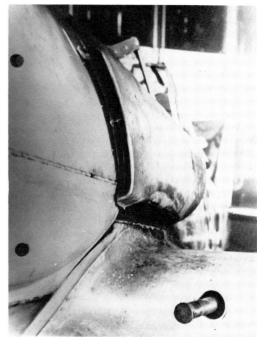

Fw 190 V43, works no. 1083, GC + LA, was equipped with the so-called *Kohlenkasten* (coal skuttle) flame shroud, and became the prototype for the planned G-3N long range night fighter bomber. In addition (right-hand photo) this aircraft had anti-dazzle exhaust shrouds on the sides of the fuselage

and then to Hexengrund torpedo establishment at Gotenhafen (Gdingen). The tests were unsatisfactory, however. The A-5/U14 had a modified fuselage ETC stores carrier, Focke-Wulf carriers under the wings and an extended tailwheel leg. Fw 190A-5/U15, no. 1282, originally had Ju 87 carriers under the wings and a modified tail. This aircraft was also to be tested as a torpedo carrier, but when the torpedo tests proved unsatisfactory this aircraft was used for carrying the Blohm & Voss Bv 246 *Hagelkorn* (hailstone) guided torpedo. Later another Fw 190G-8 was used in these experiments as well.

Number 1346, an Fw 190A-5/U16, was the first Fw 190 to have exposed MK 108s (3cm) under the wings instead of the MG 151s, MG/FFs and MK 103s built into the wings.

Fw 190A-5/U17 was an armoured ground attack aircraft that went into series production in June 1943 as the F-3. Its armament

was to be either that of the A-5/U12 or the A-5/U11.

Further variants of the A-5 were the A-5/R1, a lead aircraft, and the A-4/R1 and A-5/R6, corresponding to the A-4/R6. An A-5/R6 was tested with a WGr 28 at the Tarnewitz weapon testing station, but the tests were soon abandoned as fruitless.

Errors of navigation led to German fighter pilots accidentally landing two more Fw 190s in England and of course they fell into British hands. At night these pilots had mistaken the Thames estuary for the English Channel and Kent for France. They landed at Manston fighter base which, during the Battle of Britain in 1940, had been one of the very centres of conflict between the German and British fighters.

British long-range reconnaissance aircraft had kept a constant watch on the Focke-Wulf factories in Bremen and they estimated the monthly production of Fw 190s

Fw 190A-5/U14. works no. 871, TD + SI was one of two torpedo testing aircraft

to be 80. The Eighth USAAF decided on a daylight bombing raid on the factory and on 17 April 1943, 115 American bombers carried out the first attack in broad daylight. 16 bombers were lost and 44 others returned home badly damaged and were unserviceable for some time. When the long-range reconnaissance aircraft established that there did not seem to be any particular hurry to repair the factory, the British feared that their assumptions leading to the attack had been mistaken. Then a high-flying Spitfire on reconnaissance discovered that there were still some Fw 190s on the factory airfield, these apparently being fighters which had landed there after sorties. It was only then that the British realised that production of Fw 190s had been dispersed.

Installation of the LT 5F torpedo under Fw 190A-5/U14, works no. 872

The British were successful subsequently in striking a decisive blow against Fw 190 production capacity when, on the night of

Top: Fw 190A-5/U15, VL+FG, with Blohm & Voss
Bv 246 guided torpedo

Above: Mounting of MK 108 (30mm) on Fw 190
A-5/U16, works no. 1340

Right: Works drawing of Fw 190A-5/U15 with Bv 246

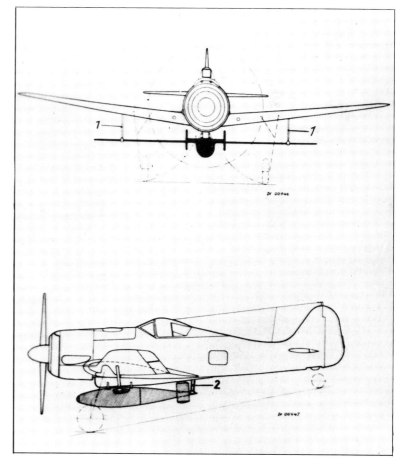

BREMEN
FOCKE-WULF WORKS
K 1038
Neg. No 23171

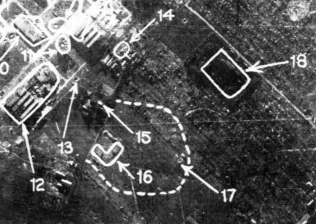

9/10 March 1943, 217 Lancasters and Hali-faxes bombed Munich. 264 bombers had taken off but 47 had been intercepted by night fighters. During the actual raid on Munich only eight of the bombers were shot down. The BMW factories in Munich suffered considerable damage and this did have a considerable effect on the production of aircraft engines.

It did not take British reconnaissance aircraft long to discover that the AGO plant at Oschersleben southwest of Magdeburg were also producing Fw 190s. The British had paid particular reconnaissance attention to the Dessau and Braunschweig area as a large proportion of the German aircraft industry was concentrated there. A raid followed on the AGO works on 28 July which seemed to have little effect on production despite 300 bombers being involved. Now the British reconnaissance aircraft started looking specifically for airfields which had Fw 190s on them. They found plenty but most of them were simply unit base airfields. Finally they discovered a large factory complex which was producing Fw 190s near Marienburg in West Prussia. This was a suitable target for the Eighth USAAF. The attack was combined with attacks on Danzig and Gotenhafen (Gdingen). Gotenhafen-Hexengrund was an important Luftwaffe testing station for free-dropping weapons, torpedoes, guided weapons and

English Reconnaissance photograph of Focke-Wulf works in Bremen before the raid in April 1944

similar devices. On 9 October 1943 378 Boeing B-17s attacked Gotenhafen, Danzig, Marienburg and Anklam, where there was an Arado subsidiary factory. The following day a Mosquito reconnaissance aircraft from Leuchars in Scotland flew to the target area and confirmed that apart from other damage, six factory hangars had been burnt out. But the cost had been the loss of 28 B-17s shot down and almost a hundred were so badly damaged that they were totally unserviceable in the immediate future.

Mention has already been made of the ill-fated raid on Schweinfurt (14 October 1943) in connection with the Fw 190A-4/R6. So far as the USAAF was concerned, the Schweinfurt failure resulted in the worst crisis of the Second World War. Yet the success of German defence forces could hardly conceal the severity of the attack and its implications: there were fifteen direct hits at Fichtel & Sachs and three hangars were in ruins. At VKF Factory I, all buildings on the west side including the power station were destroyed and at VKF Factory II, all the main buildings were totally destroyed and seven others were partially destroyed. The Speer Ministerium, Rüstung und Kriegspro-duktion (Armaments and War Production) had to recognise that 60 per cent of the total production capacity of Schweinfurt had been destroyed by this one air raid. This was the severest blow that the German aircraft manufacturers had suffered – and the consequences were to be seen in the coming months.

Fw 190A-5 trials in Japan

Japanese Fw 190A-5

6. The High Altitude Fighter - a Failure

The Fw 190's inadequate performance at altitude was a constant source of concern for Galland, General der Jagdflieger, the Technisches Amt (Technical Office of the German Air Ministry) and Focke-Wulf, the manufacturers. Officially the BMW 801 engine was supposed to produce its full power up to a height of about 22,600 ft but in fact it had difficulties at any altitude above 19,700 ft.

The Series B was a first attempt at solving the problems. Four aircraft of the A-1 series, works nos. 0046, 0047, 0048 and 0049, and one of the A-4 series, works no. 811, were converted to high altitude fighters. This conversion consisted of the installation of a pressure cabin and also the BMW 801 D-2 power plant. Number 0046 was unarmed, and nos. 0047 and 0048 both had synchronised MG 17s and two MG 151/20s in the wing roots. Number 0049 was different only in that it had an additional GM-1 power boost injection system. These four aircraft were designated B-0, whilst the A-4 modified aircraft (number 811) was designated Fw 190 V12(B-1). It was similar to number 0049 but it also had two MG/FFs in the outer wings. The manufacturers tested the five prototypes at Hanover-Langenhagen between January and August 1943. Number 0046 now had a new wing of 10.24m span and so was unarmed. After the tests at Langenhagen were complete, it was transferred to Rechlin on 9 January 1943 for test flying.

At Langenhagen test flying was mainly carried out by Chief Test Pilot Sander, but his work was hampered time and time again by the slow delivery of spares and modification parts. The problems encountered in heating the cockpit and with the cockpit canopy had not been overcome. The aircraft was unsatisfactory at altitude because the cockpit canopy glazing was not capable of withstanding cockpit differential pressure. The tests were continued up to the end of 1943 but were then abandoned in favour of the planned C series.

There were only 12 prototypes of this version built and it never went into series production. The aircraft which remained at the end of the test flying programme were modified yet again and served as prototypes for the Ta 152.

The first prototype for the planned Fw 190C version was Fw 190A-O, no. 0036, SK + JS. The Daimler-Benz DB 603A engine, which developed 1750 PS at take-off, was selected as the power plant. The new 10.24m span wing as used on the Fw 190B was also used in this aircraft. SK + JS had two MG 17s over the engine and two MG 151/20s in the wing roots. Although the turbo-supercharger intended for the C series was not yet fitted at this stage the machine already had excellent performance at altitude. Heights of over 33,000 ft were attained repeatedly. The test programme ran under the designation Fw 190 V13(C-O).

There then followed the Fw 190 V15, CF + OV, which was also a converted Fw 190A-0 (no. 0037). It was largely the same as 0036 but differed in not having a pressurised cockpit.

71

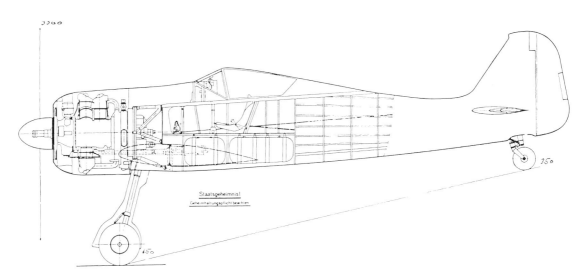

Cutaway drawing of Fw 190B

One of the first Daimler-Benz 603 engines was fitted in Fw 190 V16, CF + OW, an unarmed conversion from Fw 190A-0 (no. 0038). This engine was rated at 2,000 PS at sea level. The engine was unreliable, however, so the aircraft did not produce satisfactory results. Fw 190 V17, (no. 0039) CF + OX, suffered a similar fate. The aircraft was never completed but stored without either engine or weapons in an unpainted state.

Fw 190 V17 was followed by Fw 190 V18, CF + OY, which was also an Fw 190A-0 conversion from no. 0040, but this one used the DB 603A-1 engine. Unlike V13 which had a three-bladed propeller, V18 had a four-bladed propeller. After the first test flights the machine was converted to V18/U1 and was fitted with one of the first turbo-superchargers from the Hirth company at Stuttgart-Zuffenhausen and it was redesignated GH + KQ. The shortage of raw materials in Germany meant it was not possible to

produce a suitably heat-resistant alloy, a problem which the Americans soon solved because of the unlimited variety of raw materials freely available to them. The problems experienced by the Germans with exhaust turbo-superchargers were not overcome before the war had ended.

The next aircraft, Fw 190 V19, no. 0042, GH + KP, was to have swept-forward wings, but tests proved this to be unsatisfactory. It then received normal A-3 wings and in this form the aircraft served as a flying test bed.

Burst Fw 190B pressurised cockpit, converted from Fw 190A-0, works no. 0047

72

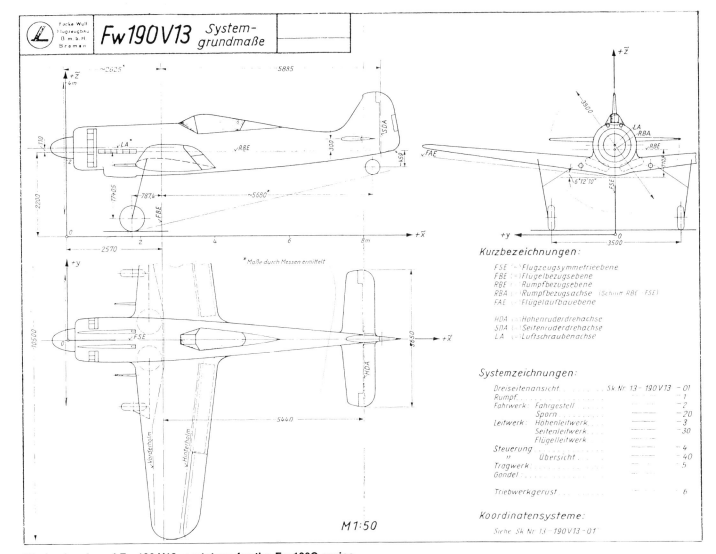

Works drawing of Fw 190 V13, prototype for the Fw 190C series

A number of engines were lined up for testing in it: BMW 801J (2000 PS), BMW P.8028 (1550 PS), DB 603 (1750 PS), DB 609 (2660 PS), DB 614 (2020 PS), DB 623 (2400 PS), Jumo 213A-1 (1740 PS), Jumo 213A-2 (1740 PS) and Jumo 213S (1750 PS). During these tests the aircraft crashed, on 16 February 1944.

The DB 603A was tested in Fw 190 V20, works no. 0043, GH + KQ, which, after the tests were abandoned, was put into storage. The same happened to Fw 190 V21, works no. 0044, GH + KR.

There then followed Fw 190 V29 which like its predecessor Fw 190 V18 was already classed as Fw 190C-1. Like the others it was a conversion from an Fw 190A-0, in this case works no. 0054. It bore the identification GH + KS and had a DB 603G power plant fitted. The other prototypes for the C-1 series (mentioned below) were also converted from the Fw 190A-1. The Fw 190 V30, GH + KT, works no. 0055, was largely similar to V29. B31, no. 0056, registration no.

73

Fw 190 V13, converted from Fw 190A-0, works no. 0036

GH + KU, was written off during test flying on 29 April 1943. Fw 190 V32, no. 0057, registration number GH + KV, never successfully completed its test flying programme because of difficulties with the DB 603G. The last prototype of the planned C-1 series, Fw 190 V33, no. 0058, registration number GH + KW, was armed with two MG 131s over the engine and two MG 151/20s in the wing roots. It crashed on 13 July 1944.

The Fw 190C-1 high altitude fighter version would probably have been an excellent aircraft for combatting high altitude bomber formations but as already mentioned it failed because it proved impossible to manufacture a reliable turbo-supercharger system. The HMZ turbo-supercharger 9-2281 produced by Hirth, kept burning out.

Daimler-Benz DB603-A engine installation in Fw 190 V13

All three versions which were fitted in the following types were unreliable in operation: He 111H-21, Do 217 V13 and V14,

Fw 190 V13, formerly Fw 190A-0, works no. 0036, was unarmed initially

Fw 190 V15 (C-0). Modified from Fw 190A-0, works no. 0037

Fw 190A-0, works no. 0038 was modified to become Fw 190 V16, CF + OW

Ju 88A-4 with Jumo 211Q, Hs 130A-0/U6, Hs 128 and He 274. The turbo-superchargers themselves worked well but the pipes which directed the engine exhaust gases to the turbo-supercharger were unable to withstand the high temperatures. A report dated 26 October 1944 states that it was impossible to increase the life expectancy of turbo-superchargers to more than 20 hours.

Fw 190A-0, works no. 0040, was modified to become Fw 190 V18, CF + OY, but unlike its predecessors in the C-0 series it had a four-bladed propeller

It was therefore a shortage of raw materials which prevented the successful development of turbo-superchargers. It was only when the Jumo 213 was available that it was

Daimler-Benz DB 603A for the planned Fw 190C-1 series

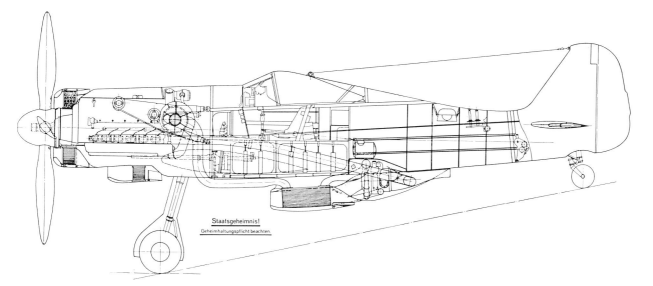

Works cutaway drawing of an Fw 190 V18/U1 fuselage

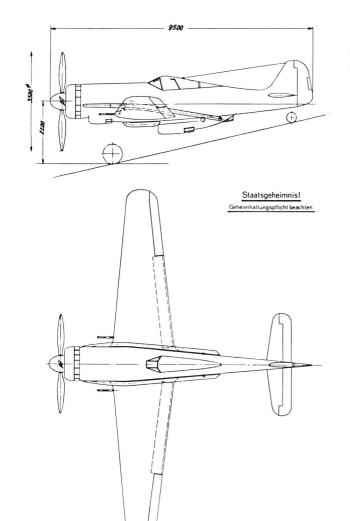

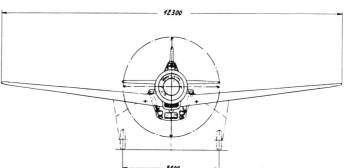

possible in the Fw 190 D and the Ta 152 to build fighters which, with ceilings of 34,500-36,000 ft, were a match for the high altitude Allied fighters. But at this point the aircraft industry in Germany was already so battered that the sort of production numbers needed to produce significant results were now impossible.

Works drawing of the Fw 190 V18/U1

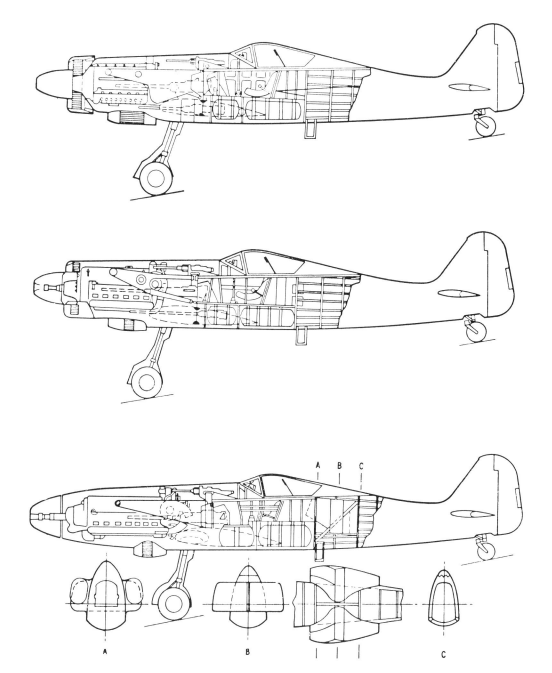

Cutaway drawings of the
fuselage of the Fw 190 V19
showing various engines.
From the top: Jumo 213 with
special radiator, DB 603
without turbo-supercharger,
DB 603 with side-coolers,
BMW 801 J

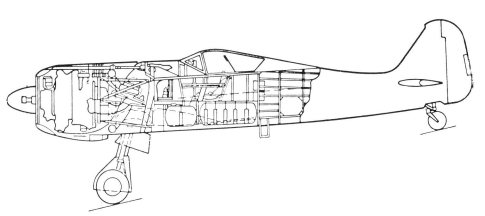

78

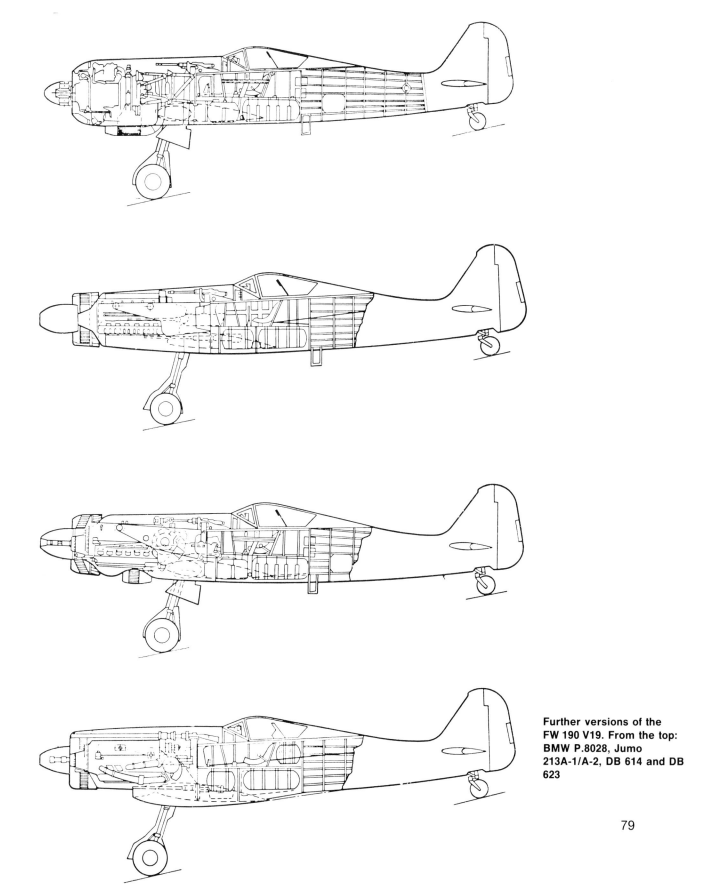

Further versions of the
FW 190 V19. From the top:
BMW P.8028, Jumo
213A-1/A-2, DB 614 and DB
623

79

7. From Fighter Bomber to Ground Attack Aircraft

Towards the end of Spring 1943 plans were under way for the production of a new version of the Fw 190, the A-6. It was planned that series production should begin as early as April but this was delayed until June following frequent air attacks by the Allies. The A-6 was conceived as a ground attack aircraft from the start because of the inadequate performance of the BMW 801D-2 at altitude. In addition to the various Focke-Wulf subsidiaries, Arado with its factories in Brandenburg and Anklam, AGO in Oschersleben and Fieseler in Kassel were to build the aircraft under licence. A total of 569 aircraft of this version were built between June and December 1943. As mentioned above the prototype for the A-6 series was the Fw 190A-5/U10, no. 861.

The Fw 190A-6 was different from the previous versions in the following respects: the wingspan was increased to 10.506m and the wing-mounted MG/FFs were replaced by MG 151/20s – in this case with a barrel without a muzzle-brake. The change in weapons resulted in a flat bulge on the upper surface of the wing. There was an ejection chute under the wing and in the outer portion of the port wing a Robot camera was installed. During series production the undercarriage main wheels were changed. The FuG 16ZE required the installation of a ring aerial on the underside of the fuselage.

The A-6/R1 was based on the Fw 190A-5/U12. It was the so-called *Pulkzerstörer* (formation destroyer) and was extremely heavily armed, having two MG 17s over the engine, two MG 151s in the wing roots, two MG 151/20s in each of the weapon pods, and WB 151s under the wings. These weapons were fitted in 60 Fw 190A-6s at Luftzeugamt Küpper. The oil cooler was particularly susceptible to gunfire, so A-6 no. 410258 was used for testing various forms of armour and this resulted in a satisfactory solution to the problem.

The Fw 190A-6/R1 aircraft built in Küpper were ready for action on 30 November 1943. They were first used in the 3 Staffel of JG 11. Only one test prototype was built of a planned A-6/R2 version and this was Fw 190 V51, works no. 530765; this was also to serve as the prototype of the A-7/R2 series at the same time. It was generally the same as the A-6 but it was armed with two MG 17s, two MG 151/20s and two MK 108s.

The Fw 190A-6/R3 was equivalent to the V51 but it had MK 103s instead of MK 108s. It is debatable whether it ever saw active service. The prototype for the A-6/R4 version was Fw 190 V45, works no. 7347, registration number RP + IU. It differed from the normal A-6 only in that it had a GM-1 power boost injection system. Chief Test Pilot Hans Sander completed its test flying programme at Langenhagen on 2 November 1944. Some Fw 190A-6s were fitted with *Sondergeräte* (SG) (special equipment). The special equipment was the SG 116 *Zellendusche* (Shower), three vertically firing MK 103s in line which fanned out at 2 degrees. Flying under an enemy formation triggered off the weapons via a photo-electric cell developed by Opta Radio. Forty Fw 190s were equipped

Fw 190A-5/U10 became prototype for the A-6 Series

Ground attack Fw 190A-6 operational in Finland

Damage following collapsed undercarriage leg to Fw 190A-6, works no. 530137. Unusually the cross is green and not black

with this weapon, and JG 10 tested it out using its own target aircraft, but it is not known whether it was ever used in action. A-6s equipped with FuG 217 radio equipment were deployed as night fighters with 1 Staffel of JG 10. When required, an ETC 501 could be added to the A-6 which could carry four SC 50s on an ER 4ZT carrier adaptor. When the fighter pilots developed the technique of attacking four-engined bombers head-on it became necessary to improve the armour round the BMW 801. For this purpose BMW modified Fw 190A-6, SM + JS and VO + LY, which were test flown from August to October 1944 in Fürstenfeldbruck.

As well as these new ground attack aircraft in the A-6 series there were, of course, still the modified versions of series A-4 and A-5 ground attack aircraft which had been developed from the F series and fighter bombers from the G series. The Fw 190F-1s were the old Fw 190A-4/U3s which in April became known as the

Close-up of push-in cockpit step

Fw 190F-1 in accordance with the revised designations. The same thing happened with the Fw 190A-5/U3 which in April 1943 became known as Fw 190F-2. On the other hand production of the Fw 190 F-3, the prototype for which had been the Fw 190A-5/U17, only began in June 1943. The armament consisted of two MG 17s and two MG 151s, and sometimes only two MG 151s in the wing roots. In addition there was an

82

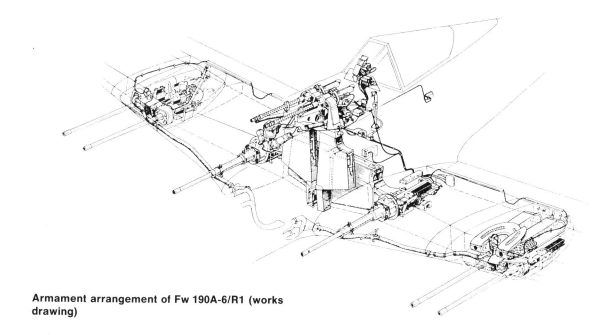

Armament arrangement of Fw 190A-6/R1 (works drawing)

ETC 501 or ETC 503 under the fuselage and two ETC 50s under each of the wings. Whilst production was already in progress the A-6 wing for the F-3 began to be equipped with the Robot camera. Fieseler built four F-3s with MK 103s, similar to the A-5/U11, and they were tested by the Luftwaffe Test Centre in Tarnewitz. This short series was to be increased to ten but was stopped. In the same way the development of an Fw 190 wing for three MG 151s was stopped by the Reichsluftministerium.

The Fw 190F-3/R1 was a lead aircraft corresponding to the A-4/R1. Some F-3s were also built with WGr 21 and known as Fw 190F-3/R6. These aircraft saw service. The basis for the Fw 190G-1 and G-2 fighter bombers had been the A-5/U8. The version with Weserflug (Ju 87) stores carriers was later renamed the Fw 190G-1. As these carriers reduced the speed of the Fw 190G-1 too much, an Fw 190A-5/U8, GH + JD, was equipped with Messerschmitt carriers. A short series was produced in this form,

known as the Fw 190G-2. Mention has already been made of the renaming of the Fw 190A-5/U2 as Fw 190G-2/N.

The fighter bomber put high loads on the undercarriage and so load testing was necessary. Appropriate tests were carried out with the Fw 190G-2, SS + GJ, and these were undertaken by Deutsche Versuchsanstalt für Luftfahrt (DVL) at Berlin-Adlershof. There were nine test landings. The sink rate was increased gradually from 5.9 ft/sec to 39.4 ft/sec and at the same time the landing speed was reduced by degrees from 114 to 107 mph. It was discovered that at a sink speed of 39.4 ft/sec and a landing speed of 107 mph the point was reached where the fuselage buckled. Production of the Fw 190G-3 series, which had been developed from the Fw 190A-5/U13, began in July 1943. This fighter was then produced until Spring 1944. All A-6, F and G versions, saw continuous service with the ground attack squadrons and SKG 10.

1943 was a year of many setbacks for the

Fw 190A-6/R1
Pulkzerstörer (bomber
formation destroyer)
with MG 151/20s in the
wing roots and two
MG 151/20s in a gun
pod under each wing

Close-up of WB 151
gun pod under wing of
FW 190A-6/R1

Fw 190 V51, works no.
530766 with MK 108 in
outer wing (Fw 190A-6/R2)

MK 108 in Fw 190

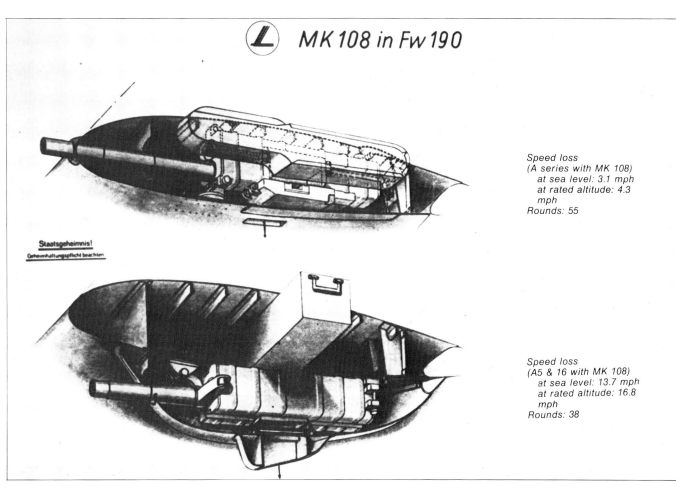

Staatsgeheimnis!
Geheimhaltungspflicht beachten

Speed loss
(A series with MK 108)
  at sea level: 3.1 mph
  at rated altitude: 4.3
  mph
Rounds: 55

Speed loss
(A5 & 16 with MK 108)
  at sea level: 13.7 mph
  at rated altitude: 16.8
  mph
Rounds: 38

Comparison of airspeed losses with MK 108 in the wing or under the wing

Luftwaffe and for the Fw 190 formations as well. Allied landings in Algeria and Tunisia had meant that SG 4 was sent there. Allied air superiority and supply difficulties caused the squadrons to dwindle. The ground attack squadrons on the Eastern Front had taken part successfully in the offensive by the 4th Panzerarmee west of Charkow. In Africa the remains of the German formations capitulated on 12/13 May 1943. A few

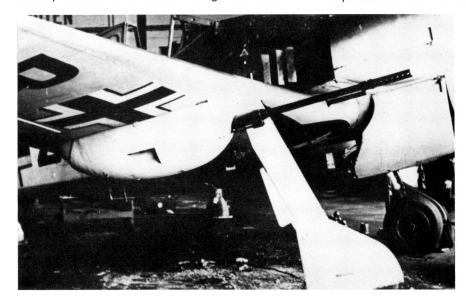

Fw 190A-6/R3 with MK 103 under outer wing

Fw 190A-6 as night fighter equipped with FuG 217 JR operational with I/JG 10

German aircraft did manage to escape to Sicily.

On 23 May 1943 SKG 10 made a low level attack on Hastings with 20 Fw 190s and on Bournemouth with 26 Fw 190s. There were heavy civilian casualities losses in Bournemouth, 127 being killed and 298 injured. On 1 June the same formation attacked Margate with 20 Fw 190s and Niton, Isle of Wight, with 10 more. Ten days later the Allied Combined Bomber Offensive began with daylight bombing raids by the Americans and night raids by the British. The main targets of this air offensive were, as agreed in Casablanca in January 1943, German fighter bases and fighter factories.

The German fighter bombers in the ground attack squadrons continued their attacks on targets in Southern England and the South-East. The ground attack aircraft and Fw 190 fighters were also engaged in operation *Zitadelle,* the offensive against the Soviet Front near Kursk and Orel. They could do nothing to prevent defeat. The landings on Sicily, which were supported by massive Allied attacks, on 9 July 1943, led to the loss of 80 per cent of the German aircraft stationed there, amongst them many Fw 190s. SG 4 carried out attacks against the bridgehead at Salerno in September but these failed because of Allied air superiority. German units suffered to the extent that on 3 September, when sections of the British Eighth Army landed on the south coast of Calabria, there were only 625 German aircraft serviceable altogether in

Fw 190A-6, VO + LY, with BMW 801S-1 undergoing tests at Fürstenfeldbruck, August-October 1944

the South of France, Italy, Sardinia and Corsica. On 15 September in the Salerno area alone seven Fw 190s were destroyed and five more were severely damaged as a result of Allied attacks on German airfields.

Fw 190A-6, SM + JS, was the second aircraft fitted with the BMW 801S-1 to be tested at Fürstenfeldbruck

Series production of the Fw 190F-1 (ground attack aircraft) at the AGO plant at Oschersleben

Fw 190F-2 ground attack aircraft. Field maintenance; changing the engine

Fw 190F-2 of I/SG 4 on the Eastern Front

The last reliable production figures for the Fw 190 are from this period, the end of September 1943. Up to this point the numbers built were as follows:

Fw 190A	3223
Fw 190F	548
Fw 190G	790
Total	4561

Tropicalised Fw 190F-2 of I/SG 4 in Central Italy, 1943

Fw 190F-3 of IV/SKG 10, Sicily, 1943

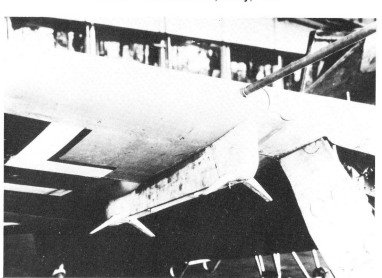

Fw 190F-3 with wing-mounted ETC 501 carrier and
MG 151/20

Fw 190F-3 of I/SG 4 in Italy, 1943

Fw 190G-2 was developed from Fw 190A-5/U8

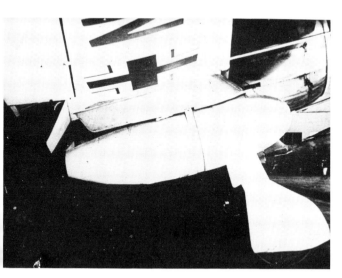

Extended range fighter bomber (Jaborei) Fw 190G-1 carried a 300 litre drop tank on a Ju87 carrier under each wing

From about the same time there is an indication of the distribution of Fw 190s in the individual units. Research has not revealed any figures for the Mediterranean area:

Eastern Front

14/JG 5	17
Staff JG 51	15
I/JG 51	32
III/JG 51	34
IV/JG 51	26
15/JG 51 (Spanish)	20
Staff JG 54	3
I/JG 54	27
II/JG 54	27
IV/JG 54	36
Staff/SG 1	1
I/SG 1	40

(together with Hs 129)

Fw 190G-3/N long-range night fighter bomber of III/KG 51 in Northern France, 1944

This Fw 190G-3, DN+FP, was captured by the Americans in Italy

The same aircraft, being test flown by the 85th Fighter Squadron in North Africa

The same aircraft once again, in German colours in the USA, 1946 (works no. 160016)

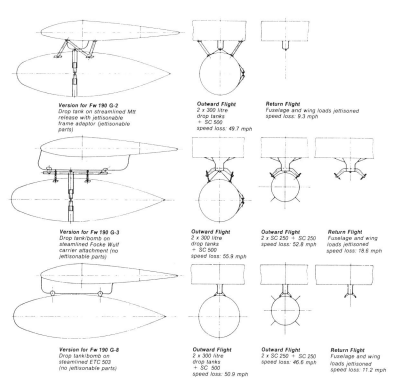

Version for Fw 190 G-2
Drop tank on streamlined Mtt release with jettisonable frame adaptor (jettisonable parts)

Version for Fw 190 G-3
Drop tank/bomb on steamlined Focke Wulf carrier attachment (no jettisonable parts)

Version for Fw 190 G-8
Drop tank/bomb on steamlined ETC 503 (no jettisonable parts)

Outward Flight
2 x 300 litre drop tanks
+ SC 500
speed loss: 49.7 mph

Return Flight
Fuselage and wing loads jettisoned
speed loss: 9.3 mph

Outward Flight
2 x 300 litre drop tanks
+ SC 500
speed loss: 55.9 mph

Outward Flight
2 x SC 250 + SC 250
speed loss: 52.8 mph

Return Flight
Fuselage and wing loads jettisoned
speed loss: 18.6 mph

Outward Flight
2 x 300 litre drop tanks
+ SC 500
speed loss: 50.9 mph

Outward Flight
2 x SC 250 + SC 250
speed loss: 46.6 mph

Return Flight
Fuselage and wing loads jettisoned
speed loss: 11.2 mph

The airspeed difference applies to climb and combat power at 2,400 rpm, at sea level and on an otherwise "clean" aircraft (Fw 190 A-5)
Speed loss caused by ETC 501 under fuselage is 7.5 mph!

Works drawings dated 20.1.44: mounting arrangements for drop tanks and bombs on Fw 190 G series aircraft

France

Luftlotte 3

Stab Aufkl	
Gruppe 13 (Staff Reconn.)	2
1/Aufkl. Gr 13	9
2/Aufkl. Gr 13	9
1/Aufkl. Gr 122	5
4/Aufkl. Fr 123	4
5/Aufkl. Gr 123	7
Stab/JG 2	8
I/JG 2	26
III/JG 2	34
Stab/JG 26	2
I/JG 26	45
II/JG 26	45
Jagdkommando Brest	5
I/SKG 10	33

Luftlotte German Reich

Stab (Staff)/JG 1	3
I/JG 1	33
II/JG 1	28
I/JG 11	44
10/JG 11	13
Stab/JG 300	4
II/JG 300	4
Stab/JG 301	2

This means that at the end of September 1943 there were approximately 650 Fw 190s operational. If we assume that there were a maximum of 100 Fw 190s operational in the Mediterranean area, that gives a total number of approximately 750 Fw 190s, in addition to which there were approximately 50 aircraft in the training schools. If we assume a total production of approximately 4500 aircraft, that means that a horrifying total of 80 per cent of the aircraft were lost between 1941 and 1943. From this can be inferred the number of dead or severely wounded pilots, and thus can be gained the impression of the high losses that the fighter pilots had suffered.

26 November 1943 saw a heavy daylight bombing raid by the Eighth USAAF on Bremen in which there was large-scale destruction of the Focke-Wulf factories. On 13 December the US 8th and 9th Air Forces bombed Kiel, Hamburg and Bremen with 1462 aircraft and in these raids Luftwaffe bases in the region and also Amsterdam-Schiphol Airport were bombed. JG 1 and JG 11 suffered heavy losses in opposing the American bomber formations. Continuing USAAF and RAF attacks constantly hindered the production of the Fw 190. Replacing machines was one thing, but replacing pilots was another.

94

Fw 190G-3 (works no. 160699) was badly damaged during an air raid by the 458th US bomber group on 9 May 1944

Fw 190G-2, SS + GJ, at the DVL in Berlin-Adlershof for load testing of the undercarriage

8. Fw 190 Operational on all Fronts

The next series, Fw 190A-7, was actually to be a reconnaissance version but in November 1943 Focke-Wulf, AGO and Fieseler began constructing the A-8 as a direct successor to the A-6. Whilst the A-8 was being produced, modifications were required at the instigation of the Technisches Amt which gave Oberingenieur Blaser sleepless nights again. What was required was the installation of FuG 16ZY, the GM-1 power boost injection system and 115 litre tanks. As 80 aircraft had already been produced in the original version by January 1944, these were now designated A-7. The prototype aircraft for this version was Fw 190 V35, no. 816.

The main difference between the A-6 and A-7 was in the installation of two MG 131s, instead of the previous MG 17s, above the engine. The considerably larger and heavier weapon produced a flat bulge on the engine cowling in front of the cockpit. Some A-7s were delivered with an MG 151/20 in the gun pod under each wing and these were known as the A-7/R1. Experimentally a version was manufactured with MK 108s instead of the MG 151s of Fw 190 V51, and this was known as the Fw 190A-7/R2. Only isolated examples saw operational service because it was not possible to get production under way until after the death of Udet, and also there was insufficient production capacity because of the scarcity of raw materials. On the other hand the Fw 190A-7/R6 with WGr 21 (corresponding to the A-4/R6) was used to good effect against American bomber formations.

It was planned that production of an Fw 190F-4 should start at the end of 1943 to supplement the ground attack versions. This version however was modified into an F-8 and its production started at the beginning of March 1944. Instead of being powered by the BMW 801F like the F-5, the Fw 190F-9 was built around the BMW 801TS. The Fw 190F-6 was to be developed from the A-6, but this project was dropped. In its place an F-10 was to be built with a new wing of increased wingspan, three MG-151s, or one MG 151 and one MK 103 in each wing. But this project was never completed either.

Things were fairly quiet in the air on the Eastern Front until about the middle of January 1944. The situation had worsened for the German fighter aircraft because the Russian fighters now had the same rate of climb as the Fw 190 and could turn more tightly. It seems probable, however, that the young Russian fighter pilots who had been rushed to the Front lacked the necessary experience to exploit these advantages. The only advantage remaining to the Fw 190 was that in a dive it was considerably faster than the Russian Lawotschkin La 5 because of its higher wing loading.

The German Jagdgruppen often transferred from the Fw 190 to the Bf 109 and vice versa. For example III Gruppe of JG 51 changed to the Fw 190 in February and March whereas I Gruppe received the Bf 109 and yielded its remaining Fw 190s to III Gruppe. But in March III Gruppe was again equipped with the Bf 109G. What did the pilots think? 'The Me 109 climbs faster than

Fw 190A-7 badly damaged by US air raid

Fw 190A-7 of JG 1 (Stab), early 1944

Fw 190A-7 in the West, 23 June 1944

Russian Lavochkin La 5-FN fighter. This type was often misidentified as an Fw 190

the Fw 190 now, but the Fw 190 is better for shooting down enemy aircraft.'

In February the US 8th Air Force increased its raids on the German aircraft and aircraft engine factories. Initially the bomber formations had little success because of unsuitable weather conditions, with the result that most of the B-17s which attacked Berlin on 22 March 1944 with Brandenburgische Motorenwerke in Spandau (where the BMW 801 was built) as their main target, could not identify their target and dropped their bombs on secondary alternative targets so BMW 801 production was hardly affected.

The fact that the Allies were now using long-range escort fighters to protect the bombers made it increasingly difficult for

Installation of MG 131 over the engine in a Fw 190

German fighters to gain access to them. However, these escort fighters had to recognise that they were now dealing with a more powerful Fw 190A, namely the Fw 190A-8

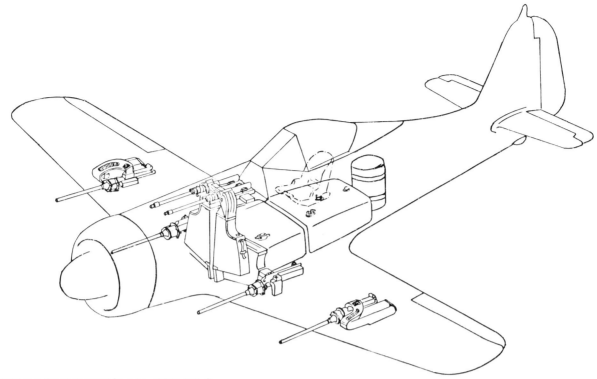

Armament arrangement in a Fw 190A-8/A-9

which was produced from February 1944 onwards.

The Fw 190A-8 was to be produced in greater numbers than any other series; in all 1344 aircraft in different versions were produced.

The main features included a pitot tube on the starboard wing tip and fuel fillers behind the cockpit for the 115 litre long-range internal fuel tanks. Incidentally this fuel tank was directly interchangeable with the GM-1 power boost injection system fuel tank. There were filler openings for the starting fuel on the port side beneath the cockpit; on the underside of the fuselage in front of the direction finding loop there was a large service hatch for the oxygen bottles; the ETC 501 was relocated 20cm forwards; under the port inner wing there was a Morane aerial for the FuG 16ZY and also a

window for a Robot camera. From January 1945 onwards the pilot's rear armour was reinforced, and in addition to that a compound curvature canopy was fitted. Because of the bottleneck at VDM-Luftschrauben (propeller manufacturers) in 1945, metal-sheathed wooden propellers produced by Junkers and also by Schwarz were fitted.

During series production a number of variants occurred as follows. The Fw 190A-8/R1 had two MG 151/20s under the wings. The drag of these weapons caused such a loss in air speed that from April 1944 they were no longer fitted.

Individual aircraft had MK 108s fitted instead of MG 151/20s (Fw 190A-8/R2). Four Fw 190A-8s were equipped as the A-8/R3 with underwing MK 103s and were put into service. An Fw 190A-6/R4 never got past the

Celebration in Finsterwalde: Fw 190A-8 after the 75th 'kill' by Major Waltern Dahl, Kommodore of JG 300

Fw 190A-8 flown by Oberfeldwebel Migge of I/NJGr 10 (night fighters) with FuG217 at Werneuchen 1944

Fw 190A-8, works no. 171683, captured by the Americans

Armoured canopy protection in Fw 190A-8

project stage; it was to be armed with a total of only four MG 151/20s. The Fw 190A-8/R5 was similar and did not get past the project stage either. R7 conversion kit equipment was available for the Sturmstaffeln (assault

squadrons) of the Jagdgeschwader. It consisted of a reinforced front windscreen and 30mm thick triangular front side panels to the canopy. In other respects it was the normal A-8, but whether this equipment was fitted as standard in series production is doubtful.

The Fw 190A-8/R8 was built in large numbers for the Sturmstaffeln and the Fw 190A-8/R and A-8/R7 were dropped in its favour. The Fw 190A-8/R8 had an additional 15mm bullet-proof windscreen and 30mm thick triangular side panels, and in addition there was armour plating in front of the instrument panel and the MK 108 magazine was also protected. In addition the cockpit canopy side panels were 30mm thick and the fuselage sides were also protected with

Fw 190A-8/R2 of 6/JG 300, Holzkirchen, September 1944
Fw 190A-8/R2; MG 151 in wing root, MK 108 in the outer section and MG 131 over the engine

Fw 190A-8/R3 with MK 103 under outer wings. The MK 103 fairing had to be extended forwards to overcome severe vibration problems

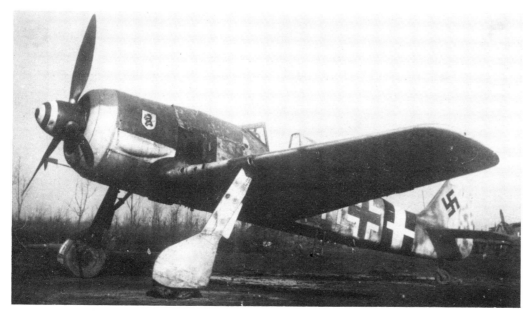

Fw 190A-8/R7 of 4 Staffel of II/JG 4 led by Major von Komatzki, used for ramming missions against US bombers

Fw 190A-8/R8 (works no. 681382) of the Sturmgruppe of JG 3 led by Hauptmann Moritz

Rear armour on Fw 190A-8/R8

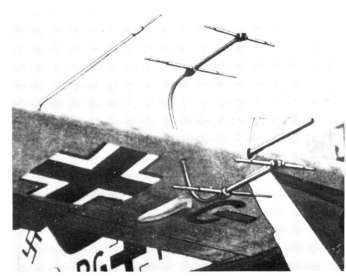

Fw 190A-8 of I/NJGr 10 testing FuG218 V1 equipment

additional armour plate. This armour could not be fitted after September 1944 because of the shortage of raw materials. From January 1945 the reinforced windscreen had to be abandoned but the armour plating at the back of the cockpit was reinforced. All this armour led to an increase in weight and

consequently the assault fighters only had MG 151s in the wing roots and the usual guns in the wings in an attempt to keep the weight down.

There was a night and all-weather fighter, the Fw 190A-8/R11, but only a few of these saw active service. This was because of

Fw 190A-8/U1 converted from a Fw 190 A-5 at Altenburg

An Fw 190A-8/U1 restored in England after the War

supply difficulties with the PKS 12 direction finder and the FuG 125 – its ring aerial rather like a direction-finding loop, was mounted on the fuselage just in front of the tail. The A-8/R11 was fitted with anti-dazzle exhaust shields and FuG 218 aerials (FuG 218 *Neptun*). It was armed with two MG 131s and four MG 151/20s.

There had been a two-seater trainer version of the Bf 109 (Bf 109G-12) but not of the Fw 190, consequently the fighter pilot school Jagdfliegerschule Altenburg had converted a few Fw 190A-5s to two-seaters using their own workshop facilities. At the end of 1944 Focke-Wulf went over their drawings and prepared two-seater modification kits, but by this time 58 two-seaters had already been produced at Altenburg. The manufacturers, however, never ran a series production of two seaters. The two

seaters produced in Altenburg were known as the Fw 190A-8/U1.

The Fw 190A-8 was also used as a flying test-bench for a whole range of special equipment. Increasing the range of aircraft meant fitting auxiliary fuel tanks but their drag made a noticeable difference to the flying speed. Attempts were made to design the auxiliary fuel tanks and attach them in such a way that the loss of speed was as small as possible. In 1944 the Graf Zeppelin Research Institute carried out experiments with auxiliary fuel tanks in the shape of streamlined bodies mounted on the upper surface of the wing. After wind tunnel tests, these were tried on two Fw 190s, an A-8 and a G-2. The test flights ran from 17 July to 23 August 1944 and the results were extremely positive. An Fw 190 wth a normally mounted and full 300 litre auxiliary fuel tank suffered a speed loss of 21 mph (7.4 per cent) whereas the same aircraft with an ETC carrier but without the fuselage-mounted auxiliary fuel tank only lost 8.5 mph (2.9 per cent). Compared with that an Fw 190 with a pair of full upper wing surface auxiliary fuel tanks (2 x 300 litres) only lost 0.9 mph (0.3 per cent). If the aircraft only had one upper surface wing tank, and that on the starboard wing, then the speed loss was an incredibly low 0.6 mph (0.2 per cent). This asymmetrical arrangement was possible because – viewed from the cockpit – the propeller turned clockwise so the weight of the upper surface fuel tank counteracted the propeller torque. By August 1944 it was too late in the war to make use of these advances.

A number of special devices were developed and tested on the Fw 190 A-8. One such device was the SG 117 *Rohrblock*. Pilots had reported that 'a salvo of fourteen 30 mm shells is the most effective way of shooting down four-engined bombers'. This weapon consisted of seven MK 108 barrels, with seven spring-loaded firing pins mounted on

a 20 mm thick plate. They were fired by an automatic electrical system at intervals of 3 to 4 milliseconds. Six Fw 190s equipped in this way were tested in combat but the results were not satisfactory.

The SG 500 *Jagdfaust* was developed by Dr Langweiler to produce a recoil-free 5 cm-calibre weapon. Tests were carried out in the August of 1944 using an Fw 190 at Brandis-Waldpohlenz airfield. It was found that he had virtually eliminated the recoil problem, and this weapon was later fitted in the Me 163; it was Me 163s equipped with the SG 500 that were used by JG 400 to defend the Leuna works in October 1944. Other 'wonder weapons' were also being developed, expecially for tank and ship attack. These developments are detailed later.

In the meantime the Fw 190A-8 had produced the F-8 ground attack aircraft. It was equipped with the so-called *Grosse Bombenelektrik* (an electrical bomb release system) for releasing bombs individually. Compared with its predecessor, the F-3, the main difference was the installation above

Tests on fuel tanks mounted directly under the wing carried out by the Graf Zeppelin research institute

Tests on upper
surface wing body

Fw 190A-8 with
two *Doppelreiter*
(double rider)
wing bodies

Fw 190A-9 of 10/JG 54 at Müncheberg near Berlin, March 1945

the engine of the MG 131s instead of the MG 17s. Up to the Autumn of 1944 there was a considerable fuselage similarity with the A-7 with its fuselage armour and undercarriage armour. Then the A-8 fuselage was equipped with a 115 litre auxiliary tank and the ETC 501 was relocated 20 cm forwards. In 1945 further modifications ensued which will be mentioned later. Developments were also well advanced on the *Jaborei* versions.

Some of the short series of the Fw 190G-3 (144 aircraft in all) which had been built from July 1943 onwards, were equipped as night fighter bombers with anti-dazzle exhaust shields or flame eliminators and landing lights. They saw service in 1944 with Nachtschlachtgruppe 20 (night ground attack) (formerly III/KG 51). In this use as ground attack aircraft the Focke-Wulf stores carriers were exchanged for two ETC 50s. This version was known as the Fw 190G-

Oberleutnant Fritz Krause, NJGr 40, testing the Fw 190A-9/R11 at Werneuchen, 1944

3/R5. Similar to the F-8 was the *Jaborei* Fw 190F-8 which was built from November 1943 to February 1944. The fuselage was that of the A-7 but without the MG 131 over the engine and the ETC 501 under the fuselage. The series was discontinued in

February with the explanation from official sources that there was no longer any need for a *Jaborei*; 146 Fw 190G-8 were converted to ground attack aircraft by exchanging stores carriers under the wings for ETC 50s. In 1944 the last of the A series the Fw 190A-9, was produced, but only a very few of these ever saw active service. Externally they were recognisable by greater radius turbo-supercharger inlet ducts and individual exhaust outlets under the fuselage. This meant that the manifold for cylinders 8 and 9 which had been under the fuselage was now unnecessary. The cooling fan for the BMW 801 F-1 now had 14 fan blades. All the aircraft in this series had a compound curvature canopy and reinforced armour protection behind the pilot.

The Fw 190A-9/R1 differed from the A-8/R1 only in that it was powered by the 2000 PS BMW 801 F-1. The same applies to versions A-9/R2 and A-9/R3.

A number of versions never got past the design stage. The A-9/R8 was to have the BMW 801TS/TM and was to be armed with two MG 151/20's in the wing roots and two MK 108s under the wings. The A-9/R11 was largely similar to the A-8/R11 but was armed with two MG 131s, two MG 151/20s and two MK 108s and was powered by the BMW 801 TS. The Fw 190A-9/R12 was similarly equipped. There was also a plan to build an Fw 190A/10 which would have resembled the A/9 in most respects except for an increased span of 20.50m. There were plans for Fw 190A-10/R1 to R3 versions, but they were never built.

The ground attack Fw 190F/9, which was also to be powered by the BMW 801TS only existed in prototype form (V35 and V36). A planned F-10 series never got beyond the

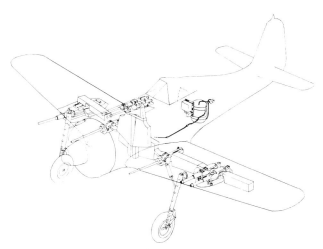

Weapon arrangement for the planned Fw 190A/10

drawing board. The Fw 190F-15 was only built as a prototype: V66, works no. 584002. It was mainly the same as F-9 but it had the inner wing of the Ta 152 and its undercarriage. In March 1945 this aircraft was flown to Rechlin for testing but it flew out there powered by the BMW 801D-2, as the BMW 801 TS was to be installed on arrival at Rechlin.

The last version of the F-series was the Fw 190F-16 of which only one was ever manufactured, the prototype V 67, works no. 930516. It was officially planned that the F-16 would have the more streamlined engine cowling of the BMW 801TS, and its turbo-supercharger inlet either on the starboard side like the D-9 or in the wing roots. The range was to be increased by the installation of 55 litre tanks in the wings. It was also to have the FuG 15 installed. One version was also required as a torpedo carrier instead of the cancelled F-17.

The Fw 190F-9/R16 was to be fitted with a TSA 11D swinging arm bomb launching system for dive bombing and the ETC 504 fuselage stores carrier. This aircraft was also to be fitted with the complete tail unit from the Ta 152. This version was never built.

9. The Long-nosed Fw 190

When powered by the BMW 801 the Fw 190 had poor performance at altitude and this led increasingly to its being used as a ground attack aircraft and fighter bomber. The development of the aircraft as a high altitude fighter powered by a Daimler-Benz engine with turbo-supercharger had failed through lack of availability of suitable turbine materials.

From the middle of 1942 onwards Junkers Motoren-Werke were producing the new high performance Jumo 213 engine, developed by Dr Lichte. It was intended originally as a bomber engine, but Dr Lichte also developed fighter versions of it, variants C and E, in which the drive systems and oil feed to the variable pitch propeller were so arranged that a tunnel was left free for weapon installation. The Jumo 213's nominal power was 1750 PS, proven through five 100 hour runs. Series production of the engine, however, was so hindered by continual Allied bombing raids that it was not until mid 1944 that these engines became available in any numbers. Consequently Professor Kurt Tank suggested that a 190 should now be powered by this engine. An old Fw 190A-0, works no. 0039, was used as the test aircraft (this aircraft had already been intended for the development of the Fw 190C). It was now modified yet again and renamed the V17/U1. This aircraft was unarmed and even during test flying was not fitted with a spinner. It came to Langenhagen in May 1944. On 4 August it was followed by Fw 190 V54, works no. 174024, BH + RX. Fw 190 V53, works no. 170003,

DU + JC, was also a converted A-8. Its test flying programme began in Langenhagen on 19 September 1944. The conversion took longer as there were MK 103s built into the wing roots.

Some indication of the outstanding performance of Oberingenieur Blaser and his team can be gained from the fact that the design drawings for the Fw 190D-9 were completed as early as March 1944. The test flying programme went so well that contracts for series construction were allocated to the Focke-Wulf factories in Cottbus and Sorau and to the Fieseler factories in Kassel. The Focke-Wulf factory commenced production in August and Fieseler in September 1944. Altogether 674 Fw 190D-9s (as the series became known) were built, starting at works no. 210001. TR + SA, works no. 210001, was test flown by Sander, the chief test pilot, on 7 September 1944, aircraft works no. 210002 on 18 September.

It was usual to fit the MW 50 power boost injection system for short-term emergency extra power. The MW 50 fuel tank could either be used for water/methanol injection or simply as a reserve fuel tank. An all-weather version, the Fw 190D-9/R11, was discontinued from 11 December 1944. As far as is known, JG 2, JG 26 and the III/JG 54 were the first fighter units to receive the Fw 190D-9. At first the pilots were not very impressed with the new aircraft. The Jumo 213 was supposed to produce 1850 PS but only produced 1750, and the fighter pilots believed that the long-nosed version of the Fw 190 was less manoeuvrable. They

Fw 190 V17/U1, converted from Fw 190A-0, was the first prototype for the long-nosed Fw 190D-9

Fw 190 V53, works no. 170003, DU+JC, was another prototype for the D series, converted from an Fw 190A-8

Fw 190 V53 at Langenhagen, early September 1944

disliked the new long-nosed version so much that Kurt Tank decided to fly to Oldenburg to visit III/JG 54 in the Autumn of 1944 to explain to them the advantages of 'Dora'. He explained to the fighter pilots: 'The Fw 190D-9 is an emergency measure until we have the Ta 152. The main factory producing the BMW 801 has been bombed. There are no other engines of this power available. There are, however, large numbers of the Jumo 213 available because of the stop on bomber production ('fighter priority programme'). We must use these engines and you will soon notice that the new aircraft really is good. I can tell you that we are now producing 4000 fighters a month. In Spring we shall be overtaking the aircraft production figures of the Allies.' The last part was a propaganda lie which few

will have believed. The pilots did not conceal their displeasure. The Commander of III/JG 54 simply said: 'Provided that this is only an interim measure. If you want us to fly 'Dora 9' we shall do so.' And fly it they did. Surprisingly, when pilots had adapted to it they could turn more tightly than in the Fw 190A or the Bf 109G. It could reach extremely high speeds in a dive and it climbed as well as anyone could wish. Nowadays former pilots who flew the Fw 190D still regard it as the best fighter of the Second World War.

On one job the Fw 190D proved to be positively unique. The Me 262 jet fighter which was already in operation was virtually defenceless during take-off and landing because of its engine characteristics. The Fw 190D-9 often flew protective patrols over

Fw 190 V56, works no. 170924, GV + CW, prototype for the D-11 series, also converted from an A-8, arrived at Longenhagen on 29 September 1944 for test flying

Installation of Jumo 213A-1 in Fw 190D-9

Me 262s taking off and landing and they were usually successful.

The Allies had a healthy respect for the Fw 190. When an Fw 190G-3 (works number 160016) fell into American hands during the fighting around Naples it was immediately transported to USAAF Materiel Command at Wright Patterson Field in the United States for precise investigation and testing. There it was test flown by Lieutenant Colonel Barney Estes. After he had flown it a few times he said: 'It's no wonder that our boys have a healthy respect for the Focke-Wulf!'

The first two aircraft produced in the series, works nos. 210001 and 210002, were to be prototypes for the new version, the Fw 190D-10, which was similar to the D-9 except that it was to have two MK 108s in the wing roots instead of the MG 151/20s. It never went into series production.

Fw 190D-9, works no. 210051
with 300 litre drop tank

Rear view of the same aircraft

Fw 190D-9 with engine cowling
and undercarriage bays open

Another modified A-8 arrived at Langenhagen on 29 September 1944 and this was to
be the prototype for the D-11 series (V-56,
works no. 170924, GV+CW). It was followed
on 29 October by Fw 190 V55, works
no. 170923, GV+CV, the second prototype
for the D-11 series. The Fw 190D-11 was to

Fw 190D-9, works no. 611444

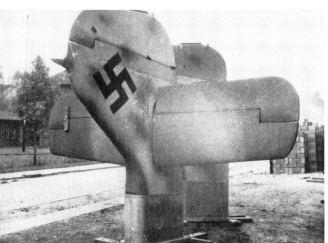

Close-up of Fw 190D-9 tail

have the same armament as the D-10, but to be powered by the Jumo 213 F. In fact there were only ever five D-11s, all converted from A-8s, all test aircraft. Of those, by 21 December 1944 the following had landed at Langenhagen:

5 Sept: V57, works no. 170926, GH + CV
9 Nov: V61, works no. 350158, VI + QM
16 Dec: V59, works no. 170933, GV + DF

Whether V58, works no. 350156, and V60, works no. 350157, were test flown has not been established. All five aircraft had the MW 50 emergency power boost injection system. The armament was not as planned but consisted of two MG 151/20s in the wing roots and two MK 108s in the outer wings. The planned all-weather fighter Fw 190D-11/ R20 and R21 did not pass the design stage.

Another Fw 190A-8, works no. 350165, was to be the prototype (V63) for the Fw 190D-12 series. A second A-8, works no. 350166 CS + IB (V64) was used as a prototype for the all-weather fighter Fw 190D-12/R11. This series was to go into production in February 1945 at Arado and in January 1945 at Fieseler. It is doubtful whether the conversion of the two proto-

115

Fw 190D-9 flown by
Oberleutnant Romm,
JG-3 photographed at
Prenzlau, March 1945

Fw 190D-9 of Stab
(staff) IV/JG 3 at
Prenzlau, March 1945

Stab Fw 190D-9 aircraft
of IV/JG 3 at Prenzlau,
March 1945

116

Fw 190D-9 landing after a sortie

Fw 190D-9, works no. 600651, which was captured by the Americans in Africa and test flown by North American Aviation

Fw 190D-12/R11, works no. 401392, probably one of the very few aircraft in this series actually produced by Fieseler

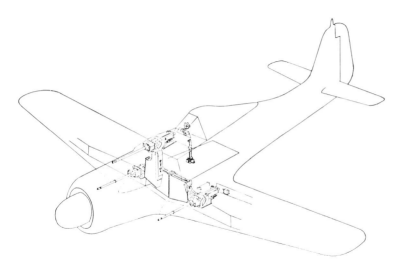

Armament arrangement of Fw 190D-9

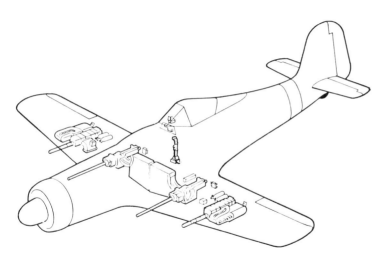

Armament arrangement of Fw 190D-11

types was ever completed and whether series production began. This type too was to be powered by the Jumo 213F-1, to have the MW 50 injection system, and to be armed with an MK 108 motor-cannon and two MG 151/20s in the wing roots, and to have FuG 125 and PKS 12 equipment fitted. The planned D-12/R5 series with increased range and D-12/R25 with modified radio equipment were never realised. A further Fw 190A-8, works no. 350167, was to be used as a prototype for the Fw 190D-12/R5 and then for the next version D-13/R5. There was no series contract for this version but for an all-weather version the D-13/R11, series production of which was to begin on a decentralised basis at the 'Roland' combine from January 1945 onwards. This version differed from the D-12 in having different armament, this being an MG 151/20 motor-cannon and two MG 151/20s in the wings. This version and the D-13/R5 and R21 planned versions never got past the drawing board. The Fw 190D-9, works no. 210040, was to be the prototype (V76) for the D-14 series, aircraft works no. 210043 (V77) and prototype for the D-15 series. Whether these two aircraft were ever converted is not known, but there was certainly no series production. The successor to the long-nosed Fw 190D was the Ta 152.

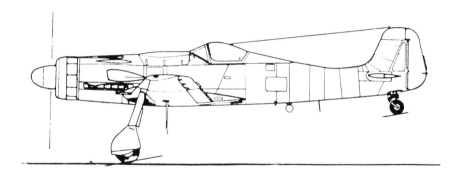

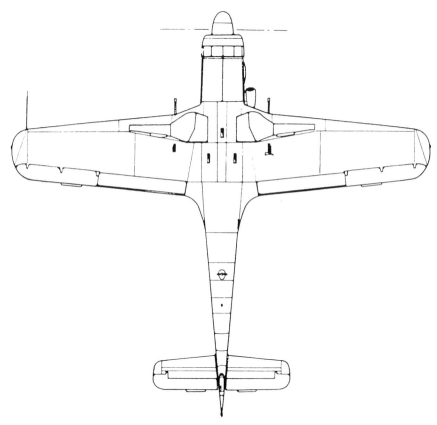

**General arrangement drawing of
Fw 190D-9**

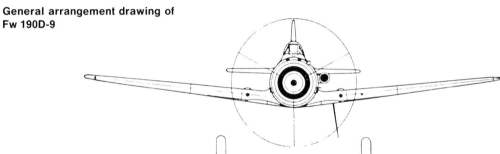

119

10. From Fw 190D to Ta 152

About the middle of 1944 Professor Kurt Tank had succeeded in ensuring that all new designs at Focke-Wulf would bear his name. Consequently there were no further Fw types – just Ta types. The new fighter was to be called the Ta 152 although it actually ought to have been called Ta 153. In the USAAF evaluation report on the documents confiscated from the Focke-Wulf factory in 1945 can be read the words: 'The Ta 153 was the prototype of the Ta 152, developed from the Fw 190. It was so different from the Fw 190 in terms of production that attention was diverted to the production of the Ta 152.' This Ta 153 had already been the subject of a discussion between Begandt (of Focke-Wulf) and Hügelschaffer (of Messerschmitt) in Augsburg on 30 July 1943, when the subject of the relative weights of the Ta 153 and the Me 209 (probably V5) was discussed). We discover from this report, amongst other things, that the Ta 153 design (referred to as the Fw 190D) was very similar to the Messerschmitt 209 but did not have a pressure cabin and did not have alloy armour plate behind the fuel tank. Neither the Me 209 nor the Ta 153 were realised (with the exception of Me 209V5, SP + LJ).

The design of the Ta 152A proceeded with the Jumo 213A and flame eliminator shroud system, but this was not realised either. It was preferable to modify prototypes from the stored Fw 190C test aircraft in order to save development and construction time.

The fact that between the end of 1944 and the end of the war no Ta 152 test aircraft had been built has meant that it is very difficult to gain an overview of the development of the Ta 152. There is for example an Fw 190 V20/U1 as prototype for the Ta 152C-0 and a Ta 152 V20 as a prototype for the Ta 152C-3.

The most urgent need was for a high performance high altitude fighter so the first priority was to develop the Ta 152 H, easily recognised by its high-aspect ratio wings with a span of 14.44m, which increased the wing area to 23.5sq m. But the development of the Ta 152H-0 seemed ill-fated. The first prototype, the Fw 190 V33/U1, was ready at the beginning of July 1944. It was the old Fw 190A-0, works no. 0058, GH + KW, which had already served as prototype for the C series. It had been equipped with a new engine, the Jumo 213 E-1, but was still unarmed. It took off from Langenhagen on 12 July 1944 for its maiden flight, but was totally written off in a crash the next day. The next aircraft, the Fw 190 V30/U1, works no. 0055, GH + KT, did not do much better. It took off for its maiden flight on 6 August 1944 and after one week was a total write-off in a crash on 13 August! It was only with the third prototype, Fw 190 V29/U1, works no. 0054, GH + KS, that test flying was completed without any major problems. Sander took off for the maiden flight on 23 September 1944. The test results were positive and a pre-series Ta 152H-0 contract was awarded and these aircraft were to be delivered in October and November 1944 although the test flying of the prototype was still incomplete. On 18 October, Fw 190 V18/U2,

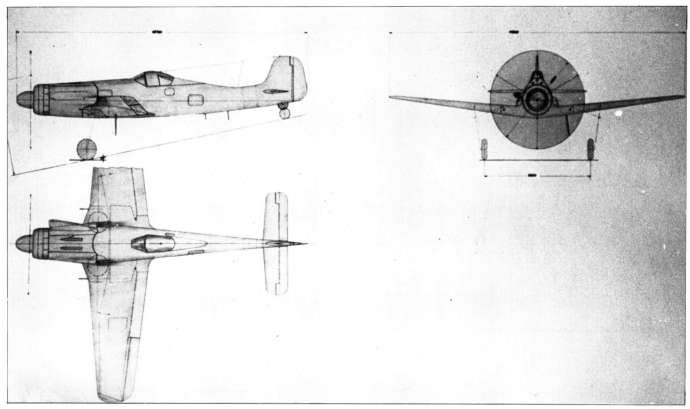

Works drawing of the Ta 152A which was never built

Planned armament and fuel arrangements for Ta 152

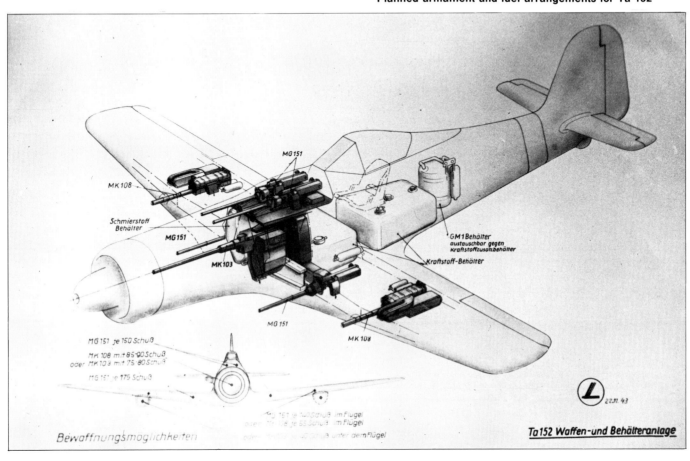

MG 151

MK 108

Schmierstoff
Behälter

MG 151

MK 103

MG 151

MK 108

GM 1 Behälter
austauschbar gegen
Kraftstoffzusatzbehälter

Kraftstoff-Behälter

MG 151 je 150 Schuß

MK 108 mit 85-90 Schuß
oder MK 103 mit 75-80 Schuß

MG 151 je 175 Schuß

Bewaffnungsmöglichkeiten

22.11.43

Ta 152 Waffen- und Behälteranlage

Close-up of Fw
190 V20/U1, converted
from Fw 190A-0, works
no. 0043

the old CF+OY, now designated GH+KO, works no. 0040, took off on its maiden flight. On 11 November 1944 it crash-landed in a field and was of no further use for test flying. In the meantime people were working feverishly to produce the Ta 152H. The last prototype, the Fw 190 V32/U1, works no. 0057, GH+KV, received the improved wing which was intended for the Ta 152 V25. By the middle of December 1944 its test

The same aircraft as above, Langenhagen, October 1944

Fw 190 V21/U1, works no. 0044, GH+KR, with DB 603E engine
Fw 190 V29/U1, works no. 0054, GH+KS. Chief Test Pilot Sander's successful flight in this aircraft on 23 September 1944 counted as the first flight of the Ta 152

Fw 190 V29/U1 with three-blade propeller

Fw 190 V30/U1, works no. 0055, GH + KT, crashed on 13 August 1944 and was a write-off

flying was still incomplete as it was still in Hanover-Langenhagen on 17 December 1944. All these first five prototypes were unarmed. The pre-series Ta 152H-0 was armed with an MK 108 motor-cannon and two MG 151/20s in the wing roots. The first Ta 152H-0s were immediately delivered for operational evaluation to fighter formations in north west Germany. Kurt Tank himself had an opportunity at the end of 1944 to experience the performance of the new fighter first hand. He was flying a Ta 152H-0 from Langenhagen to Cottbus for discussions with the head of the Cottbus factory,

Front view of Fw 190 V30/U1, first prototype of Ta 152H, showing the huge 14.44m wingspan of this type

Side view of 190 Fw 190 V30/U1

Dipl. Ing. Gieschen. It was a fully equipped Ta 152 but the aircraft had no ammunition on board, in spite of a direction received shortly before from Generalfeldmarschall Milch who had warned him never to fly without ammunition. Soon after taking off from Langenhagen he heard the base station announce 'Four Indians at the garden fence!' This was code for four enemy aircraft approaching the airfield. The four Mustangs were already there and were attacking Professor Tank as he took off. Tank pressed the MW 50 emergency power boost button and within seconds the Ta 152 was roaring off and the four Mustang pilots had a good tail view of it as it disappeared in the distance. They could not match its superior performance.

A former fighter pilot, H.D. Fritzsche, told the author about his experiences with the Ta 152H. Even after the war he was very enthusiastic about the machine in which two or three days after the Armistice in 1945 he had made low-level attacks against British formations, and he commented that the aircraft was faster than any Allied aircraft at altitudes above 33,000ft and yet at lower levels handled as well as a glider.

125

TA 152H-0, works no. 150003, was test flown on 3 December 1944 by Sander at Cottbus

A few Ta 152H-1 aircraft were actually produced in series at Focke Wulf in January 1945. It is not certain whether the other contracts for the Erla factories in Leipzig and the Gothaer-Waggon-Fabrik for delivery from March 1945 onwards ever came to fruition. Very few examples were built of the all-weather version, the Ta 152H-1/R11 and H-0/R11, equipped with FuG 125, FuG 16ZY and the LGW K23 fighter control unit. One or two Ta 152H-1s were modified and fitted with the DB 603L with a turbo-supercharger intercooler.

In the meantime the construction of prototypes for the Ta 152B series had been

TA 152H-0 cockpit

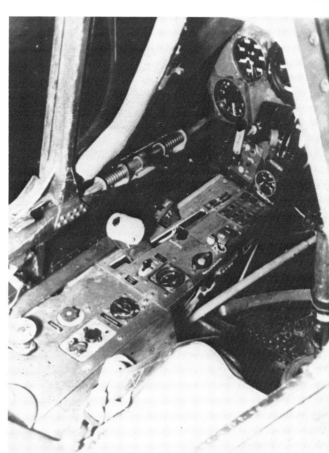

Ta 152H-1, works
no. 11005, on the
compass-swinging
turntable at Cottbus

Ta 152H-1 of JG 301
(Stab)

Ta 152H-1, works
no. 150162, at
Langenhagen,
Spring 1945

Works no. 150003 was captured intact by the British at Langenhagen in 1945

completed. The first test prototype was the Fw 190 V53, the prototype for the D-9 series which was now powered by the Jumo 213E, armed with an MK 103 motor-cannon and two MK 103s in the wing roots. This was now tested as Fw 190 V68, works no. 170003, DU + JC.

The second prototype for the Ta 152B series was to be the Ta 152 V19, works no. 110019. As the aircraft was finished only in March 1945 it was produced immediately in the B-5/R11 version. Unlike the Fw 190 V68 which had a wingspan of 10.506m, this had a new wing of 11m span. The engine was the Jumo 213E. Its armament consisted of an MK 103 motor-cannon and two MK 103s in the wing roots. The radio equipment was FuG 16ZY and Fug 125. It is doubtful whether it was ever test flown.

In October and November 1944 the first two prototypes for the planned C series were completed. They were the old Fw 190A-0s, works nos. 0043 and 0044, which were now designated Fw 190 V20/U1 and V21/U1, GH + KQ and GH + KR respectively. Powered by the DB 603 L, their armament was one MK 108 motor-cannon and two MG 151s in the wing roots and the outer wings. Both belonged to the Ta 152C-0 pre-series. The third prototype, Ta 152 V6, works no. 110006, VH + EY, was completed on 2 December 1944. Its maiden flight was on 17 December 1944 and unlike its two predecessors it was powered by the DB 603 LA. Four weeks later Ta 152 V7, works no. 110007, CI + XM, was to follow as the prototype of the Ta 152C-0/R11 all-weather fighter. Its test flying programme began on 10 March 1945 at Langenhagen. It

128

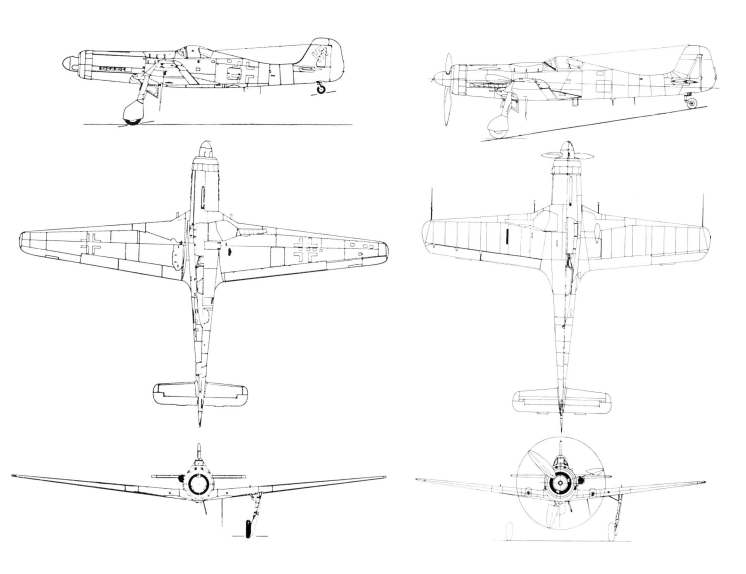

General arrangement drawing of Ta 152H

General arrangement drawing of Ta 152C

was designed for use as a torpedo carrier but by this time the torpedo testing station at Gotenhafen-Hexengrund had already been lost as the Soviet troops had advanced as far as Pomerania and so it could not be tested as planned. The next prototype of the C-0 series was the Ta 152 V8, designated Ta 152C-0/EZ because it had the Revi EZ 42 sight installed (works no. 110008). All further

prototypes of the C series, the planned Ta 152 V9 to V15 and V18 were cancelled. Production of the proven Ta 152C-1 series was to begin in May 1945, by the 'Roland' combine of Fieseler, ATG and Siebel but, in fact, only a few Ta 152C-1s were built in February and March 1945 by the Mitteldeutsche Metallwerke. According to plan these were to be supplied from the start as

Fw 190 V69 became the first prototype of the Ta 152B series, being converted from V53, works no. 170003

Ta 152C-1/R11 all-weather fighters with FuG 125 and LGW K 23. Whether that actually happened is debatable because of the difficult supply situation affecting the guidance equipment.

The next series was to be the Ta 152C-3, following the cancellation of the C-2 series in favour of C-1. The prototypes for the all-weather fighter version of C-3/R11 were to be: Ta 152 V16, works no. 110016, V17, works no. 110017, V27, works no. 150027 and V28, works no. 150030. These were to be armed with an MK 103 motor-cannon and four MG 151/20s. They were to be powered by the DB 603LA and series construction was to start at the Siebel factories in June and at ATG in July 1945. As Germany surrendered at the beginning of May 1945 that never happened.

The same thing happened with the planned Ta 152C-4 series, for which the prototypes were to be Ta 152 V22, V23 and V24. Nor for that matter was the planned Ta 152E-1 reconnaissance series in the form of Ta 152 V9 and V14 ever realised either. They were different from the C series in that

Side view of Fw 190 V68, DU + JC

Ta 152 V7, works no. 110007, CI + XM, prototype for the Ta 152C-0/R11 series. It first flew on 27 January 1945

Rear view of the same aircraft

they had the Jumo 213E engine with MW 50 injection, a Rb 75/30 topographic camera and were armed with one MK 108 motorcannon and two MG 151s in the wing roots. They were to be built by the Mitteldeutsche Metallwerke in Erfurt. A two-seater trainer version, Ta 152S-1, which was to be built by Blohm & Voss and by Deutsche Lufthansa in Prague remained wishful thinking!

And that ends the history of the Focke-Wulf Fw 190 and the Ta 152. All that remains are the ideas which were still alive in the creative mind of Kurt Tank, the designer.

11. The Very Last

In the closing months of 1944 desperate attempts were made to develop new weapons with which to combat Allied superiority. Mention has already been made of the SG special equipment for attacking bomber formations. Of equal concern were the enemy tanks in particular those of the Russians. There were also attempts to produce anti-shipping weapons which would be more effective, cheaper and more reliable than torpedoes. The Fw 190F-8 was the preferred aircraft for testing these 'wonder weapons'. Fw 190 V67, works no. 930516, was to be the prototype of a torpedo-carrying Fw 190F-16 and was completed at the end of 1944. It was fitted with 55 litre tanks in the outer wing, the TSA II D aiming device and also the ETC 504 as torpedo carrier. Testing was still incomplete when the war finished.

Tests were also carried out using Fw 190F-8-mounted flame-throwers for ground attack. The tests were discontinued, however. The SG113A *Förstersonde* was developed as an anti-tank weapon.

The Luftfahrtforschungsanstalt (Air Research Institute) at Brunswick-Völkenrode suggested a vertically firing weapon using electro-magnetic triggering. This 77 mm calibre weapon was installed in a Henschel Hs 129 and also in Fw 190F-8 W.Nr. 5782071, DR + MH. Lüneburg Heath in Northern Germany was the test site for various trigger mechanisms in January 1945 and then development was transferred to Wolfersdorf near Jena. In 18 January 1945 the top deck armour of a Pz.Kw.V Panther tank and an American Sherman tank were pierced successfully. The SG 113A never saw operational service, however. Another weapon which was tested on the Fw 190F-8 was the *Fliegende Panzerschreck*, the normal infantry weapon which, by the simple addition of a sleeve containing rocket propellant, was transformed into a rocket. Field workshops mounted rockets of this type under the wings of the Fw 190 in fours and eights. These were fitted from the barrel of a tank gun. The official name of this device was *PD 8,8 cm, Pz. Büchsenrohr.*

A similar weapon was *Panzerblitz 1.* This consisted of 8cm rocket grenades such as were used on the ground in multiple launchers, with a shell 323mm long with propellant. Some Fw 190F-8s had a jettisonable eight-rail carrier on which the rockets were hung. The rockets disturbed each other's flight paths because of their exhaust gases when a salvo was fired, so the Fw 190 had to reduce speed to about 304 mph before firing. That of course increased the risk of the Fw 190's being shot down by ground fire. The answer to this problem was the development of *Panzerblitz 2,* in which R4M rockets were fitted with a powder chamber. As the rockets were slow only a small number were produced and they were used on Fw 190F-9s from December 1944 in blocks of 12 and 14. These rockets could pierce 18 cm armour plate. A *Panzerblitz 3* was also under development but never saw operational use. There were never enough aircraft to carry these weapons and their use could hardly delay the advance of the

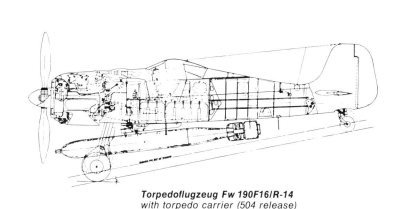

Torpedoflugzeug Fw 190F16/R-14
with torpedo carrier (504 release)

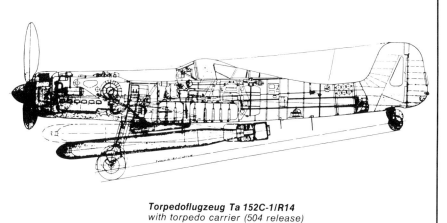

Torpedoflugzeug Ta 152C-1/R14
with torpedo carrier (504 release)
with integral 504 release
without extended tailwheel leg

Planned torpedo carrying versions of Fw 190F and Ta 152C

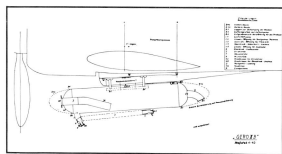

Gero IIa flame thrower installation for Fw 190

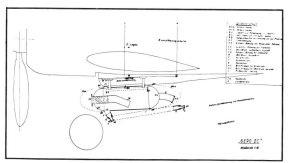

Gero IIB flame thrower installation for Fw 190

Gero IIC flame thrower installation for Fw 190

Soviet tanks. In the spring of 1943 Dr Benecke of the C/LT section of Technische Luftrüstung with the Generalluftzeugmeister (Director General of Luftwaffe - Equipment) suggested producing an aircraft-launched torpedo, preferably non-powered, which could be manufactured as rapidly and cheaply as possible. High water entry speed required a straight course under water. The Snay section of the Graf Zeppelin Research Establishment in Stuttgart-Ruit developed a

weapon to these requirements in seven sizes, BT 200 to BT 1850.

The advantage of such a weapon is clearly apparent for unlike the normal LTF5 torpedo which took 2000 man hours to produce, the BT 400, for example, only required 60 working hours, and yet carried the same warhead (200 kg). Seven BT 400s were tried out on an FW190F-8/R16 and the BT 1400 was also tested on FW190F-8/R15 and F-8/U2. After operational trials this

Fw 190 V75, works no. 582071, test aircraft for Sondergerät (SG) 113 special equipment

development was discontinued in February 1945.

It was also intended that X-4 *Jägerrakete* (fighter rocket) should be used on the Fw190. This rocket had been developed by Dr Kramer of the DVL together with Ruhrstahl-AG. The BMW 109-548 rocket motor with 8.5 kp thrust was to power it and the weight totalled 60 kg of which 20 kg was explosive. Development work began in 1942 under the GL/C-Nr. 8-344. The first 2m long X-4 was fired from an Fw190 on 1 August

Rear view of same aircraft, and (right) close-up of weapon mounted vertically in the wing of Fw 190 V75

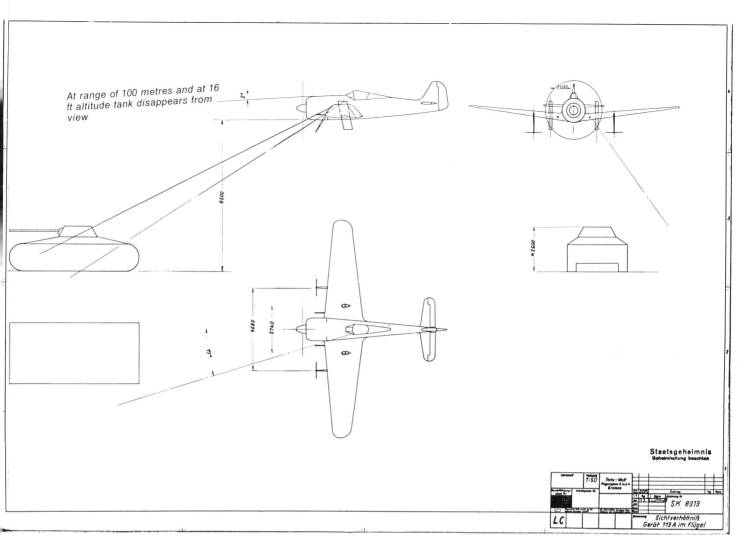

At range of 100 metres and at 16 ft altitude tank disappears from view

SK 8313

LC

Sichtverhöltniß
Gerät 113 A im Flügel

**Works drawing SK 8313
for the installation of
SG 113A in the Fw 190**

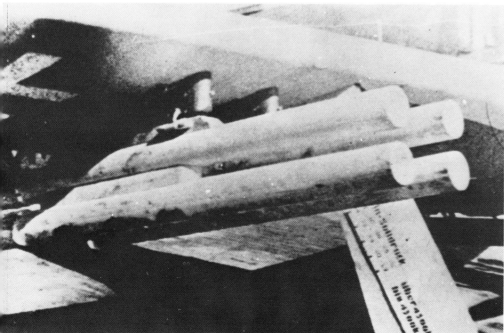

**Fw 190A-8, works no.
580303, with four PD 8.8
rockets (RPzBGr 4322)**

135

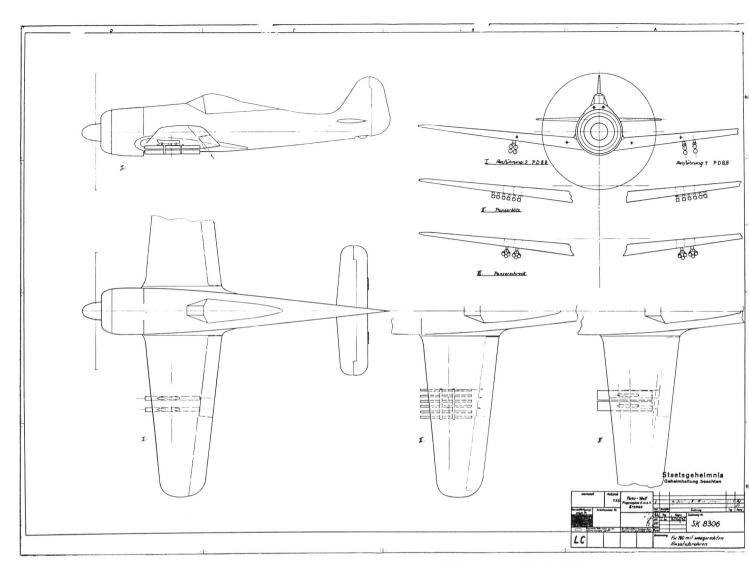

Works drawing SK 8306 for installation of PD 8.8 *Panzerblitz* **and** *Panzerschreck* **in Fw 190**

1944. Between August and December 1944 several thousand rockets were produced by Ruhrstahl but were not used as production of the rocket in the BMW factory in Stargard in Pomerania was halted through bomb damage. A few test launchings were carried out at Karlshagen test centre up to February 1945. Ju 88G-1s and Ju 388s were also equipped with its but then development had to be suspended.

Like the X-4, the X-7 rocket (also devel-oped by Dr Kramer) was wire guided. The X-7, known as *Rotkäppchen* (Little Red Riding Hood), resembled a 15cm shell with 2 wings and an offset tail. The guide wire containers were on the wing tips as in the X-4. The X-7 weighed 9kg, was 75.8 cm long and had a wing span of 60cm. Approxi-mately 300 were produced. Series produc-tion was planned at Ruhrstal in Brackwede and at Mechanische Werke in Neubranden-burg. There were Fw 190 test firings at

Karlshagen but it never saw operational service. A large number of test prototypes was discovered by the Allies in 1945 in an 'Aladdin's Cave' near Stolberg in the Harz mountains.

The Leba testing station in Pomerania was also the scene of Fw 190 tests in 1944; the SB 800 RS *Kurt* rolling bomb for use on water was test launched a number of times. The DVL and the Graf Zeppelin test establishment designed it and Dr Lambrich of Rheinmetall-Borsig (airborne weapons design) was commissioned to produce it. *Kurt* was 1.9m long and weighed 780 kg; 560 were produced, but it never saw operational service.

In December 1944 the German Luftwaffe still had over 1858 Fw 190s. Because of missing documentation it is not possible to give any details on the aircraft in Italy. The aircraft in Luftkommandos West and Luftflotte Reich were distributed as follows:

Fw 190 F-8 with vertically firing SG 116

Fw 190 with two wire-guided X-4 rockets (8-344)

Nahaufklär-		IV (Sturm) JG 3	
ungsgruppe 13		(assault)	56
(short-range		JG 4/Stab	4
reconn.)	16	11 (Sturm)/JG4	54
JG 1/Stab (staff)	4	JG 6/Stab	3
I/JG 1	36	1/JG 6	65
II/JG 1	28	JG 11/Stab	7
JG 2/Stab	4	I/JG 11	54
I/JG 2	68	III/JG 11	77
III/JG 2	45	JG 301/Stab	6
JG 26/Stab	3	I/JG 301	52
I/JG 26	81	II/JG 301	34
II/JG 26	41	III/JG 301	36
III/JG 26	77	JG 4/Stab	1
IV/JG 54	44	I/JG 4	37
JG 300/Stab	6	II/JG 4	35
II/JG 300	37	III/JG 4	44
JG 3/Stab (staff)	5		

Nachtsch-
lachtgruppe 20   40
(night ground attack)

In addition the following aircraft were on the Eastern front and in Norway:

III/JG 5	20	JG 54/Stab	1
IV/JG 5	20	I/JG 54	34

II/JG 54	44	III/SG 3	37
SG 1/Stab	5	10/SG 3	6
I/SG 1	39	SG 10/Stab	3
III/SG 1	38	1/SG 10	21
10/SG 1	6	II/SG 10	27
SG 2/Stab	8	III/SG 10	28
I/SG 2	37	SG 77/Stab	6
II/SG 2	25	I/SG 77	40
SG 3/Stab	8	II/SG 77	42
I/SG 3	49	III/SG 77	42
II/SG 3	35		

The very first day of 1945 was not an auspicious one for the Fw 190 and the Me 109: they suffered heavy losses. The occasion was Operation *Bodenplatte* (Baseplate) which was designed to take the pressure off the army groups in the west. A total of 1,035 German fighters, fighter bombers and ground attack aircraft attacked Allied airfields in Southern Holland, Belgium and Northern France and they succeeded in shooting down, or destroying on the ground, 479 Allied aircraft, 352 of them single-engined aircraft, but at some cost. 277 German aircraft were shot down, almost two-thirds of them by German flack near the V1 launching station who had not been warned of Operation Bodenplatte. When the German fighter bombers and ground attack aircraft came in low the flak fired at them with everything they had, with predictable results.

The terrible cost of this operation is apparent in the returns for the middle of January. Of the 1,858 Fw 190s listed at the end of December 1944 only 1,534 survived to the middle January 1945. From now on the German fighters were on the run. As soon as aircraft came out from under the protection of camouflage on the airfields (camouflage

which was changed frequently), Spitfires, Typhoons and Thunderbolts were on them. The ground attack aircraft and fighter bombers were reduced to operating only at night as a rule. The fighters did, however, manage one last desperate attempt. Operation Werwolf began on 7 April 1945 when 183 Fw 190A-8/R8s ramming fighters from IV (JG3), 11 (JG4), 11 (JG 300) and the special 'Elbe' group, protected by Me 362 jet fighters, JG 7 and 1/KG 54 (J) took off on a ramming mission. They attacked a massive US 8th Air Force bomber formation over Steinhuder Lake (west of Hanover) and made the ultimate sacrifice by ramming the B-17s. Twenty-three B-17s crashed, and 28 others were shot down by Me 262s, but 133 Fw 190F-8/R8s on the ramming mission were lost and 77 pilots killed. In its death throes the Luftwaffe had reared up one last time.

The Focke-Wulf test base airfield at Hanover-Langenhagen saw the last Fw190 test flight on 6 April 1945 when chief test pilot Sander took off in the Fw 190A-8, factory No. 737705, which was now Fw 190 V73, TX + PQ.

That concludes the development of the Fw 190/TA 152. Probably the last aircraft which Sander tested at Langenhagen were:

3.11.1944	Fw 190 V72	Works no. 170727 GV + BB (with BMW 801TU)
29.11.1944	Ta 152H	Wks no. 150002
3.12.1944	Ta 152H	Wks no. 150003
17.12.1944	Ta 152H	Wks no. 150004 CW + CD

1945: the end. Fw 190 components at the entrance to the underground factory at Gevelsberg, May 1945

9.1.1945	Fw 190	Wks no. 586586 NZ + QB
1.2.1945	Ta 152H	Wks no. 150030
13.2.1945	Fw 190	Wks no. 960714 RO + HR

There were other flights between then and the 6 April but they were not noted in the log book at Langenhagen.

An abandoned 'Mistel' (Mistletoe) composite, unmanned Ju 88G-1 with Fw 190A-6 as control aircraft, Karup Grove, Denmark, 1945

An American looking at Fw 190 remains at Gevelsberg, 1945

These deceptive Fw190 wooden mock-ups were photographed by American troops on the edge of St. Trond airfield, Belgium, 3 October 1944

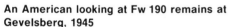

12. Tank's Dreams for the Fw190

As early as 1942 Tank had designed a jet-engined version of the Fw 190. It was to be powered by an engine developed by Focke-Wulf with a two-stage radial compressor, combustion chamber and single-stage turbine, the jet exhaust exiting at the rear. The take-off weight was designed to be 3762 kg and it was to be armed with an MG 17 and two MG 151s. It had a calculated maximum speed of 467 mph at sea level and 512 mph at 29,000 ft. The rate of climb was calculated as 531 feet per minute at sea level and 252 feet per minute at 29,000 ft. It was to have an endurance of 90 minutes flying time.

Other designs were created in connection with the Fw 190B and Fw 190C high altitude fighters including a high altitude fighter powered by the DB 603 with turbo-supercharger which had an increased wing span (wing span: 12.3m; length 9.5m; wing area 20.3 sq m).

This aircraft was to be armed with two MG 151/20s in the wing roots and two more in the outer wings. There was also to be a high altitude fighter powered by the DB 603G with double turbo-supercharger wing span 14.4m; length 11.44m; wing area 34 sq m). Another high altitude fighter proposed was similar to the one mentioned above but with a TKL 15 turbo-supercharger, and was to be 11.32m long. There was to be a fighter aircraft powered by the Jumo 222A/B (wing span 10.5m; length 11.47m; armament, two MG 131s over the engine, two MG 151/20s in the wing roots; calculated maximum speed 435 mph).

A similar design but powered by the Jumo 222C was intended to reach 460 mph. This was an aerodynamically sophisticated design with the 2500 PS BMW 802 and a propeller spinner similar to the first version of the Fw 190 V1; it had two MK 108s in the wing roots (wing span 13m; length 11.15m; wing area 34.5 sq m).

As part of the *Mistel* (Mistletoe) programme the Fw 190A-8 was equipped as the command aircraft to radio control the Ju 88G or H lower half of the composite. It was also planned to use a further composite consisting of an Fw 190A-8 and Ta 154A as a *Pulkzerstörer* (formation destroyer).

Three different versions were considered including the Ta 154, which was to be dived on its target, was to carry 2500, 3000 and 3500kg of explosives. As a result the take-off weight of the Ta 154 increased from 9930kg to 10430kg and 11030kg. In addition there was the weight of the Fw 190A-8 (excluding the armament weight) of 4100kg. These 'Mistletoe' composites would have had a take-off weight of 14030kg, 14630kg or 15130kg. No test aircraft was constructed.

It is known that most of the composites using the Me 109 or Fw 190 as the upper part and the Ju 88G or H as the lower part never saw active service although at the Junkers-Werft Leipzig altogether 125 Ju 88gs and Hs were modified for 'Mistletoe' operations and delivered to Nordhausen. Together the Gothaer Waggonfabrik in conjunction with the Deutschen Forschungsanstalt für Segelflug (DFS) developed Projects P.56 and P.57 which were to use the Fw 190 or Ta 152. This

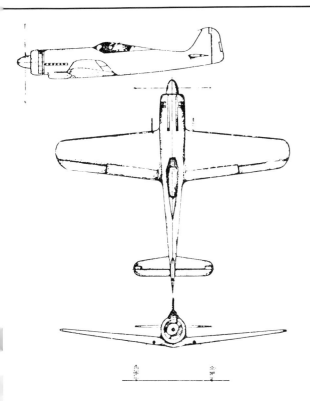

Fw 190 project with DB 603 or DB 614

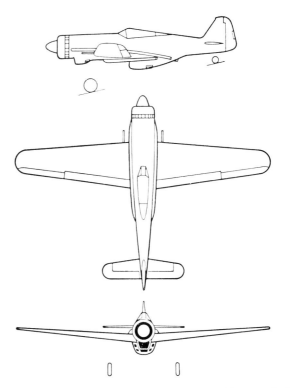

Fw 190 project for high altitude fighter with extended wing span and exhaust turbo-supercharger

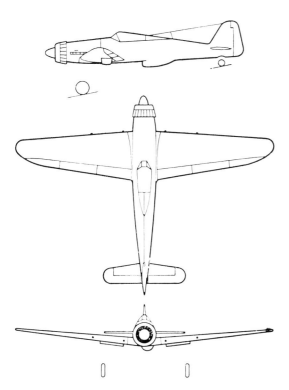

Fw 190 project for high altitude fighter with DB 603

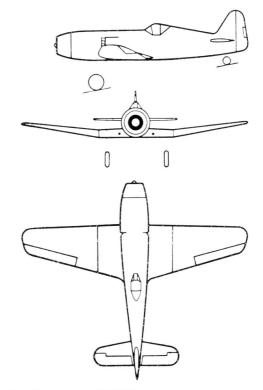

Fw 190 project with BMW 802

project centred around towed gliders which took the form of reserve fuel tanks, explosives carriers or as parasite fighters. The P.56 was a lightly armoured fuel tank glider, with a wingspan of 5.18m, and a V tail. There was a metal skid on the underside of the container glider, which was to be towed by an Fw 190A-5, attached by two wires of 6.6m length. After taking-off behind the Fw 190 it was designed to fly above it. The aim was to produce a considerable improvement in the range of the Fw 190 by using this device. The test flying institute of the DFS carried out the tests using an Fw 190B which had been placed at their disposal. A number of accidents occurred during the test flights, however, and the tests were abandoned. The Gotha P.57 was a glider bomb with wings and cruciform tail. The dimensions were approximately the same as for the P.56. No record was found as to whether this was ever tested, though a Ta 152C was intended as the test tug.

An unusual solution to the problem of producing a high altitude fighter is to be found in a design based on the Fw 190A-3. This aircraft was to have a BMW 801D-2 with four-bladed propeller and under the fuselage at the front it was to have a so-called 'strap-on turbo-supercharger'. The pressurised cockpit was armoured, though the fuel tank was not, and two MG 151/20s were mounted in the wing roots. It was calculated to have a take-off weight of 4000kg, and it was intended that the aircraft should have the 20.3sq m wing which was intended for both the other high altitude fighters. This design had to be cancelled because the turbo-supercharger tests did not produce the required results because of the shortage of raw materials already mentioned.

The last projects were two versions of the Ta 152C powered by the Jumo 222. The first version was to have the Jumo 222A/B, the second the Jumo 222E/F. Both versions were to be equipped with MG 151/20s in the wing roots and two further ones in the outer wing and both had a wingspan of 11m. The first version was 10.62m long, the second one was 10.67m. The height of the first was 4.18m and of the second 4.20m. In both cases the wing area was 19.6sq m. The all-up weight of the first version was 4900kg, and of the second version 5000kg. Both projects were cancelled as the Jumo 222 never went into series production.

At the end of 1944 there was a further high-altitude fighter project under development using the BMW 803 which was very similar to the design equipped with the BMW 802. The BMW 803 was to produce 3900 PS and this aircraft was to be armed with four MG 151/20s. At a take-off weight of 7500kg it was calculated that it would achieve 453 mph at 29,500 ft.

All these projects remained designers' dreams. The only tangible indications that the Fw 190 ever existed are the few remaining examples, some of which have been restored, in England, the United States, France and South Africa.

In Germany there is not a single Fw 190 left.

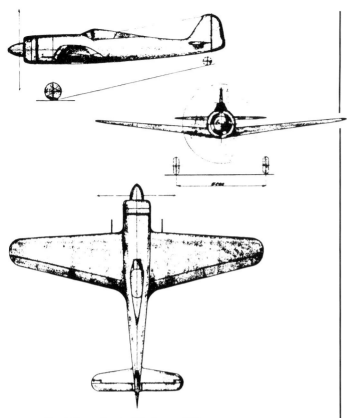

Fw 190 project with Jumo 222

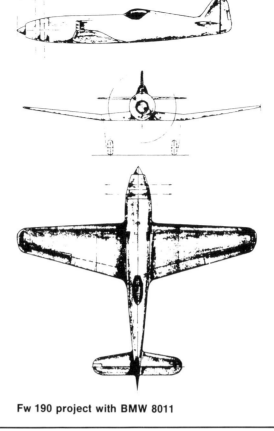

Fw 190 project with BMW 8011

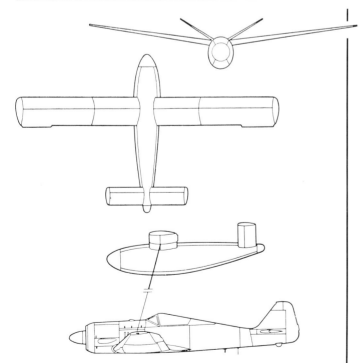

Fw 190 project with Gotha P.56 glider as parasite fighter, towed fuel tank or glider bomb

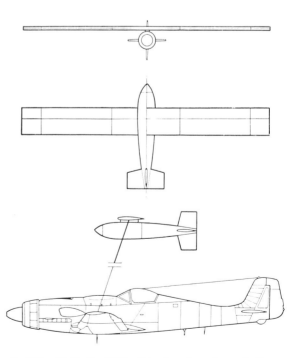

Ta 152 with Gotha P.57 glider bomb on tow, similar to P.56

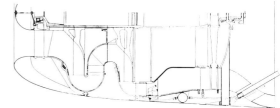

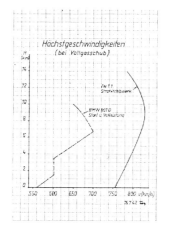

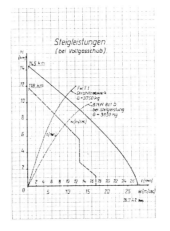

All up weight:	3750 kg
Wing area:	18.3 sq m
Armament:	2 MG 151, 2 MG 17
Armour:	93 kg
Duration:	1hr 12 mins
Fuel capacity:	1,400 litres
Fuel consumption:	1,170 litres/hour

The Focke-Wulf jet engine is installed in the existing FW 190 airframe

Fw 190 jet fighter project

Swept wing/tailpane Fw 190 project

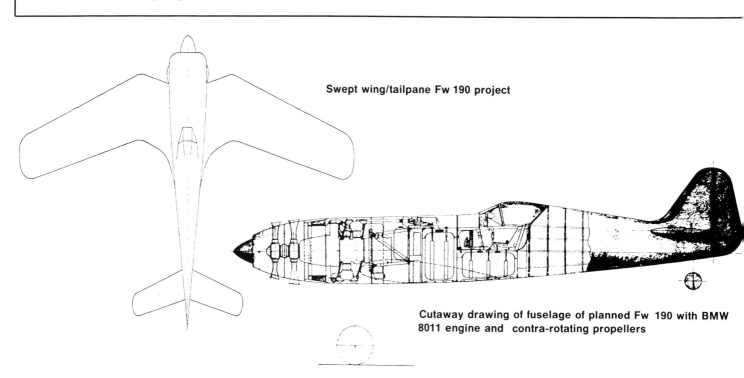

Cutaway drawing of fuselage of planned Fw 190 with BMW 8011 engine and contra-rotating propellers

Appendices

1. Focke-Wulf Fw 190

V 1	D-OPZE, redesignated FO + LY after engine modification: BMW 139 (1500 PS); wingspan: 9.515m; length: 8.85m, wing area 14.9sq m; works no. 01, unarmed
V 2	Similar to FO + LY, but 2 MG 17, 2 MG 131, FuG VIIa, works no. 02
V 3	Similar to V2, works no. 03, BMW 801A (clockwise rotation)
V 4	Similar to V3, works no. 04, BMW 801B (anti-clockwise rotation)
A-0	Works no. 0016-17, 0019-20, 0024-29, 0031-34; wing area 18.3sq m; BMW 801C-0 or C-1, FuG VIIa, 2 MG/FF, 4 MG 17
A-0/U1	(V5 and V6), works nos. 0005-6; wing area 14.9 sq m; BMW 801 C-1, 4 MG 17
A-0/U2	(V8 and V14) works no. 0008 + 0014; BMW 801D, 2 MG 131, 2 MG 17
A-0/U3	Works no. 0021; wing area 18.3sq m; BMW 801C-1, 2 MG/FF, 4 MG 17, FuG VIIa, FuG 25
A-0/U4	Works no. 0022-23; wing area 18.3sq m; BMW 801C-1, 2 MG/FF, 4 MG 17, FuG VIIa, SC 250 and 300 litre auxiliary fuel tank
A-0/U5	Works no. 0018; similar to U4, but only 2 MG 151M 2 MG 17
A-0/U6	Was to take the American Wright engine. Not built
A-0/U7	Was to be fitted with the BMW 801D engine, but not built because of non-availability of engine
A-0/U8	Works no. 0020; similar to A-0/U7 but improved BMW 801D
A-0/U9	Was to be fitted with the BMW 801C-1, but not built because of non-availability of engines
A-0/U10	Works no. 0030; BMW 801C-1, 2 MG 17, 1 MG 151, 2 MG/FF-C-2
A-0/U11	Works no. 0015; BMW 801 C-1, 2 MG/FF, 4 MG 17, undercarriage A-2 series
V 5	Replaced by A-0 pre-series
V 6	Similar to A-0 but only 2 MG 17; wing area 14.9sq m
V 7	Similar to A-0, but BMW 801C-1, and FuG VIIa and FuG 25
V 8	Similar to V7, like V7 prototype for A-1 series
V 9	Similar to V7, also prototype for A-1 series
A-1	As V7, works No. 290.0110.002-102
A-1/U1	Similar to A-1, but BMW 801D, 2 MG/FF, FuG VIIa, FuG 25
V 14	Similar to V7, but BMW 801C-2 and 2 MG 17, 2 MG 151, FuG VII, FuG 25, works no. (0120)201, prototype for A-2 series
A-2	Similar to A-1, but BMW 801C-2 and 2 MG 17, 2 MG 151, 2 MG/FF; 426 built 1941/42 at Focke-Wulf, AGO and Arado factories; operational service with II, III & IV/JG 1, I, II & III/JG 2; I/JG 5, IV/JG 5; I, II & III/JG 26
A-2/U1	Similar to A-2, but auxiliary fuel tank 300 litres, works no. 315, registration CM + CN
A-2/U3	Armoured ground attack aircraft, normal panels replaced with heavier duty steel panels, 12 built during 1942
A-3	Similar to A-2, but BMW 801D and *Kiemenspalten* cooling gills, 509 built (series 0130) during 1941-43 at Focke-Wulf, AGO, Arado and Fieseler factories
A-3/U1	Only one prototype, works no. (0130) 270, registration PG + PY. Engine relocated forwards. Later trials with Fw stores carriers under the wings. This made it the prototype for A-5 and A-5/U13 series
A-3/U2	Works no. (0130) 386; wingspan 8.798m; testing of RZ 65 rockets
A-3/U3	Works no. (0130) 300; prototype for A-3/U4 series
A-3/U3	Works no. (0130) 511; prototype for A-2/U3 series, tested in Chalais-Meudon wind tunnel
A-3/U4	Similar to works no. (0130) 300; reconnaissance aircraft with 2 Rb 12.5/7x9.5, 12 built and used by 9(H)/LG 2
A-3/U7	High-altitude fighter, only three built: works nos. 528, 530 and 531. External *Kiemenklappen* cooling flaps. Armament, only two wing-mounted MG 151/20
Aa-3	Export version for Turkey, similar to A-3, but only 4 MG 17 and 2 MG/FF
A-4	Similar to A-3, but new fixed tail surface with short mast for FuG 17. 50 aircraft (works nos. 711-760) tropicalised. 906 aircraft built between June 1942 and January 1943, armament 2 MG 17, 2 MG 151, 2 MG/FF; FuG 16Z and FuG 25 radio; operational with JG 1, 2, 5, 11, 26, 51, 54, 300, SKG 10, SG 1 and 2, FAGr 123 and NAGr 13
A-4/U1	Similar to A-4, but BMW 801C-2, operational with SKG 10
A-4/U3	Similar to A-4/U1, but BMW 801D-2, heavier armour, Robot camera
A-4/U4	Similar to A-4/U4, but FuG 17 radio and additional Robot camera

A-4/U8	Fighter bomber with extended range *(Jaborei)*. Prototypes (works nos. 669 and 670) built 1942. 300 litre tanks under wings, streamlined Weserflug (Ju 87) bomb carrier. Armament only 2 wing-root-mounted MG 151/20. Semi-circular cutouts in landing flaps. Redesignated Fw 190G-1 in August 1943, but not identical with G-1 series.
A-4	Works no. 665; trials with armour installation from 7.9.1943
A-4/R1	Similar to A-4, but 2 MG 17, 2 MG 151, 2 MG/FF and 500kg bombs, FuG 16Z-E radio, 300 litre auxiliary fuel tank
A-4/R6	Similar to A-4/R1, but 2 WGr 21 and FuG 16Z radio
A-5	Similar to A-3/U1, armament as A-4/R1, EKa 16; 723 built
A-5	Works no. 783; trials with night equipment
A-5/U1	Similar to A-5, but BMW 801C-2
A-5k	Similar to A-5, but V 5k wing (9.50m span); perhaps 10 built
A-5/U2	Works no. 711; prototype. Then ten other A-5/U8 and A-5/U13 converted to long-range night fighter bombers. Used by SKG 10. In April 1943 redesignated G-2/N
A-5/U2	Similar to A-5, works no. 783. Converted from 5 A-5/U8 and A-5/U13 to night fighter bomber with increased range. 500kg bombs and 2 300 litre drop tanks
A-5	Works no. 711; used for trials with night equipment
A-5/U3	Ground attack aircraft; armament as A-4, 500kg bombs, prototype for F-2 series
A-5/U4	Fighter reconnaissance aircraft, similar to A-4/U4
A-5/U8	Long-range fighter bomber, armament. only 2 MG 151/20, FuG 16Z radio, prototype for G-2 series
A-5/U9	Works nos. 812 and 816. Wingspan 10.506m; length 8.95m; 2 MG 131, 2 MG 151/20, 2 MG 151/20, 500kg bombs, prototype for A-7, A-8 and F-8 series
A-5/U10	Works nos. 861 and 862; prototypes for the A-6 series. MG/FF in outer wing replaced by MG 151/20
A-5/U11	Similar to A-5/U10, but MK 103 instead of MG 151/20 in outer wing. Works no. 1303 prototype for A-8/R3, F-3/R3 and F-8/R3
A-5/U12	Prototypes works nos. 813 (BH+CC) and 814 (BH+CD); 2 MG 17, 6 MG 151/20; predecessor of the A-7/R1 series
A-5/U13	Long range fighter bomber, only prototypes: V43, works no. 817, V42, works
A-5/U14	no. 1083 and V44, works no. 855. Planned for the G-1 series
A-5/U14	Torpedo aircraft. Works no. 871 (TD+SI) and 872 transferred to Hexengrund Test Centre May 1943. Possibly three other prototypes built
A-5/U15	Torpedo carrier; test aircraft works no. 1282, Weserflug bomb carrier under wings, extended tail wheel, increased fin/rudder area
A-5/U16	Prototype, works no. 1340, *Pulkzerstörer* (bomber formation destroyer), armed 2 MG 17, 2 MG 151/20, 2 MG/FF, 2 MK 108. Trials Tarnewitz, August 1943
A-5/U17	Armoured ground attack aircraft, similar to A-5/U14, but 2 MG 17, 6 MG 151/20 or 4 MG 151/20, 2 MK 103
A-5/R1	Similar to A-4, but FuG 16Z, FuG 25a radio
A-5/R6	Similar to A-4/R6, but FuG 16Z, FuG 25a radio
A-6	Ground attack aircraft; wingspan 10.506m; 2 MG 17, 4 MG 151/20, FuG 16Z, FuG 25 radio. Series built at Arado, Fieseler and AGO plants from June 1943; 569 built, some tropicalised
A-6/R1	Similar to A-5/U12; 60 aircraft converted from A-6s at Luftzeugamt Küpper (Sagan)
A-6/R2	Similar to A-6, but 2 MG 17, 2 MG 151/20, 2 MK 108
A-6/R3	Similar to A-6/R2, but MK 103 instead of MK 108
V 45	Works no. 7347; prototype for A-6/R4, July 1944
A-6/R4	Largely the same as A-6
A-6/R6	Similar to A-6, but in addition 2 WGr 21
V 34	Works no. 410230; BMW 801F and BMW 801TS engine trials 14.8.44 Rechlin
V 35	Works no. 816; BMW 801F and BMW 801TS engine trials 8.4.44 at Rechlin
A-7	Similar to A-6, but MG 131 instead of MG 17; 80 aircraft constructed from December 1943 to January 1944
A-7/R1	Similar to A-7, additional 2 MG 151/20; project
A-7/R2	Similar to A-7, but 2 MG 151/20 replaced by MK 108; project
A-7/R6	Similar to A-7. but WGr 21 under outer wing
V 51	Works no. 530765; prototype for A-8 series
A-8	Heavy fighter; 1334 machines built from February 1944
A-8	Works no. 170002; test aircraft for ramming aircraft (suicide mission) with MK 113A (5.5cm calibre), FuG 16Z-Y, FuG 25 radio

A-8/U1	Conversion to fighter trainer, two-seater, also designated Fw 190S. Altogether 58 A-5 and A-8 converted in Altenburg to Fw 190 S. Armament, just 2 MG 131
A-8/R1	Similar to A-8 but 2 MG 131, 6 MG 151/20
A-8/R2	Similar to A-8. but 2 MG 131, 2 MG 151/20, 2 MK 108; project
A-8/R3	Similar to A-8/R2, but MK 103 instead of MK 108, 4 aircraft trialled at Tarnewitz
A-8/R3	Similar to A-8/R2, but MK 103 instead of MK 108, project
A-8/R4	Similar to A-8/R1, but armament just 4 MG 151/20
A-8/R6	Similar to A-8, but WGr 21 installed in 50 per cent of the series
A-8/R7	Similar to A-8, but cockpit armour reinforced for Sturmstaffeln (assault)
A-8/R8	Similar to A-8/R2, but reinforced armour
A-8/R11	Similar to A-8. but BMW 801TU (2000 PS) and FuG 125 instead of 25 and PKS 12. Armament: 2 MG 131, 4 MG 151/20. Few of these became operational because of production problems with PKS 12 and FuG 125
A-8/R12	Similar to A-8/R11, but armament as A-8/R2. Project only
V-36	Prototype for A-9 and F-9 series
A-9	Similar to A-8, but BMW 801F-1 (2000 PS)
A-9/R1	Similar to A-8/R1, but BMW 801F-1 (2000 PS)
A-9/R2	Similar to A-8/R2, but BMW 801F-1 (2000 PS)
A-9/R3	Similar to A-8/R3, but BMW 801F-1 (2000 PS)
A-9/R8	Similar to A-9, but BMW 801TS/TM (2000 PS), armament only 2 MG 151/20, 2 MK 108; project
A-9/R11	Similar to A-9/R8, but BMW 801TS and additionally 2 MG 131
A-9/R12	Similar to A-9/R8, but additionally 2 MG 131; both projects
A-10	Similar to A-9, but wingspan 20.50m; project only
A-10/R1 to R3	The same as R-9/R1 to R3 planned, no proof that they were ever built
B-O	High altitude fighter with BMW 801D-2 and pressurised cockpit. Converted from A-1, works no. 0046, unarmed. Works nos. 0047 and 0048 with 2 MG 17 and 2 MG 151/20. Works no. 0049 with GM-1 emergency injection power boost
V 12	Single B-1, works no. 811, similar to works no. 0049, but additionally 2 MG/FF
V 13	(C-0) works no. 36, SK+JS, DB 603 A,
V 15	wingspan 10.24m; 2 MG 17, 2 MG 151/20 (C-0) works no. 37, CF+OV, similar to V13 but pressurised cockpit
V 16	(C-0) works no. 38 CF + OW, but DB 603 G, unarmed
V 17	Works no. 0039, CF+OX, unarmed
V 18	(C-1) works no. 40, CF+OY, similar to V16
V 19	Works no. 0042; converted from A-1, GH+KP; swept-forward wings, crashed 16.2.1944. Fuselage with normal wings was to serve as a test aircraft for the following engines: BMW 801J (2000 PS), BMW 0.8028 (1550 PS), DB 603 (1750 PS), DB 609 (2660 PS), DB 614 (2020 PS), DB 623 (2400 PS), Jumo 213A-1 (1740 PS), Jumo 213A-2 (1740 PS) and Jumo 213S (1750 PS). Tests discontinued
V 20	(C-1) works no. 0043, GH+KQ, DB 603, unarmed
V 21	(C-1) works no. 0044, GH+KR, DB 603, unarmed
V 29	(C-1) works no. 54, GH+KS, similar to V18, became the prototype for TA 152H-O, unarmed
V 30	(C-1) works no. 55, GH+KT, as V29
V 31	(C-1) works no. 56, GH+KU, as V30. Written off in crash 29.4.1943
V 32	(C-1) works no. 57, GH+KV, as V31, converted to TA 152 H
V 33	(C-1) works no. 58, GH+KW, as V32, crashed 13.7.1944, armament: 2 MG 131, 2 MG 151/20
V 17	Works no. 0039; unarmed, Jumo 213, converted in May 1944 to:
V 17/U1	Prototype for D-9 series
V 53	Works no. 170003; prototype for D-9 and D-10 series, June 1944
V 54	Works no. 174024; prototype for D-9 and D-10 series, July 1944
D-9	Fighter with Jumo 213A (1750 PS), wingspan 10.50m; length to 10.24m; wing area 18.3sq m; 2 MG 131, 2 MG 151/20; series construction started works no. 210001; 674 built in all
D-9/R11	All-weather fighter with extended radio equipment, production ceased on 11.12.1944
D-10	Only works nos. 210001 and 210002, 2 MG 151/20, 2 MK 108, similar to D-9
V 55	Works no. 170923; prototype for D-11 series. Jumo 213F, July 1944
V 56	Works no. 170924 as V55
D-11	Only five Fw 190A-8 (works nos. 170926, 170933, 350156, 350157 and 350158) as Fw

	190 V57, V58, V59, V60 and V61 to D-11, Jumo 213F-1, 2 MG 151/20, 2 MK 108; built in January 1945
D-11/R20	Project only
D-11/R21	Project only
V 63	Works no. 350165, prototype for D-12 series, converted from A-8
V 64	Works no. 350166, prototype for D-12/R11 series
V 65	Works no. 350167, prototype for D-12/R5 (4 wing tanks)
D-12/R11	All-weather fighter, Jumo 213F-1, 1 MK 108, 2 MG 151/20, MW 50 power boost, FuG 125, PKS 12; series construction at Arado February 1945 and at Fieseler plant January 1945 planned but no output
D-12/R5	Project only
D-12/R25	Project only
V 62	Works no. 732053, prototype for D-13 series, November 1944
V 71	Works no. 732054, prototype for D-13 series, November 1944
D-13/R5	Project only
D-13/R21	Project only
V 76	Works no. 210040, converted from D-9 to D-14
V 77	Works no 210043, converted from D-9 to D-14
D-14	Project only
E-1	Fighter reconnaisance aircraft with BMW 801 D-2, project only, replaced by A-3/U4, A-4/U4 and A-5/U4 ground attack aircraft
F-1	Ground attack aircraft, BMW 801D-2, 2 MG 17s, 2 MG 151/2s; 30 aircraft constructed in 1942
F-2	Similar to F-1, but ETC 501, ER 4, 4 SC 50; 271 aircraft constructed 1942/43
F-3	Similar ro F-2, but 4 ETC 50 instead of ETC 501; 247 aircraft constructed 1943
F-3/R1	Similar to F-3, constructed at Arado plant up to May 1943
F-3/R3	Similar to A-5/U11; three aircraft constructed December 1943/January 1944
F-4	Similar to F-1, but in addition 2 MK 103; built at Arado plant 1944
F-5	Similar to F-3, 2 MG 131, 2 MG 151/20, 1 ETC 501, 2 ETC 50; constructed at Fieseler and Arado plants 1944
F-8	Similar to F-3 but 2 MG 131, 2 MG 151/20, 2 ETC 50, FuG 16Z-Y up to March 1944 then FuG 16Z-S; C-3 emergency injection power boosts; construction began March 1944 at Arado plant, April 1944 at NDW; 385 built (NDW = Norddeutsche Dornier-werke)
V 69	Works no. 582072; 1 test aircraft for the wire controlled X4 *Ruhrstahl* rockets. F-8 (Works no. 583431, 583438 and 584221) and V70 (Works no. 530025) were also used for these tests
V 74	Works no. 733713; test aircraft for the SG 117 *Rohrblock:* vertical salvo of 7 MK 108
V 78	Works no. 551103 test aircraft for AG 140 bomb release
V 79	Works no. 581304; same purpose as V78
V 80	Works no. 586600; as above, all three converted from F-8
F-8/R1	Similar to F-8, but 4 ETC 50 under the wings, later ETC 71, delivery August 1944
F-8/R2	Similar to F-8, but 2 MK 108 cannons under the wings, only two aircraft built (NDW) no series production
F-8/R3	Similar to F-8/R2, but MK 103 instead of MK 108, only 2 aircraft built (NDW), no series production
F-8/U1	Long range fighter bomber. Wing mounted ETC 50 replaced by ETC 503 for SC 250 bombs. 300 litre drop tank under the fuselage mounted on ETC 501
F-8/U2	Used for tests of BT 1400 *Bombentorpe-dos.* 2 ETC 503s for 300 litre drop tanks, TSA 11A aiming device. Converted at Menibum works November 1944 to March 1945, no series production, replaced by F-8/R15 and R 16
F-8/R13	Night ground attack aircraft, 2 MG 151/20, 2 wing mounted ETC 503s for 300 litre drop tanks. Radio equipment : FuG 25, FuG 16Z-S, FuG 101 and PKS 12. Works no. 586597. Series production at Flug-zeugbau Klemm works never started
F-8/R14	Torpedo fighter, lengthened tailwheel leg, fuselage reinforced at former 4, ETC 502 torpedo release, without 115 litre fuselage tank. Only one aircraft, series production at Weserflug works never started
F-8/R15	Test aircraft for Bombentorpedo BT 1400, similar to R13. Simpler version of the F-8/U3: a few aircraft were allocated to III/KG 200. Series production at Blohm and Voss works never started
F-8/R16	Test aircraft for Bombentorpedo BT 700, similar to R 13, TSA IIA, aiming device, series production at Blohm and Voss works was never started
F-3	Only prototypes V35 and V36 (see A-7/A-8)
F-10	Project only
F-15	Only prototype V66 (Works no. 584002) March 1945 powered by BMW 801TS

F-16	Prototype V67 only (Works no. 930516) end of 1944; 55 litre drop tanks under outer wing. TSA IID aiming device was to be fitted as intended for torpedo carrying. R 13 radio equipment extended by addition of FuG 15
G-1	Fighter bomber with increased range *Jaborei*. Similar to A-5/U8. 2 x 300 litre drop tanks on Weserflug releases under the wings. 2 MG 151/20, ETC 501 under fuselage; 49 aircraft constructed 1942/43
G-2	*Jaborei* similar to G-1, but Messerschmitt stores carrier instead of Weserflug; 601 aircraft built 1942/43, saw service with SG 4 and SG 10
G-2N	Similar to A-5/U2, only a few aircraft built, saw service with SG 10
G-3	Similar to A-5/U13, 140 aircraft built at Focke-Wulf plant July/August 1943
G-3/R5	Ground attack aircraft, converted from G-8; 4 wing mounted ETC 50 instead of Messerschmitt stores carriers
G-3N	Conversion for night operations using field modification kits 116 and 128. Additional PKS 11 course control
G-4tp	Similar to G-3, but tropicalised, only one prototype
G-8	Fuselage modified for installation of 115 litre tank or GM-1. Fug 16Z-Y relocated further forwards, ETC 501 relocated 20 cm. further forwards under the fuselage. Only a few of these aircraft were built, November 1943 to February 1944
G-8/R5	Converted from G-8 and corresponding to G-3/R5
S	Two-seater training fighter. No series production, replaced by A-5/U1 and A-8/U1. A-5 conversions designated S-5.

Special Versions

A-8	Works no. 380394; test aircraft for *Doppelreiter* (double rider) upper wing surface fuel tanks
A-6	Works no. 7347 (V45); converted to high altitude fighter with 12.3 metre span
A-8	Works no. 530115 (V47); converted to high altitude fighter with 12.3 metre span
V 52	Works no. 170002, DU + JB (also known as V72) test aircraft for FuG 125 'Hermine'. Maiden flight 30.8.1944
V 72	Works no. 170727 GV + BB, test aircraft for BMW 801TS and PKS 12
V 73	Works no. 733705, used for testing tank busting bombs
V 75	Works no. 582071, used for testing SG 113A, a fixed anti-tank weapon, mounted vertically
F-8	Used for testing SG 116 rigidly mounted weapon firing vertically upwards. 40 machines tested with JG 10
V 25	Works no. 50, used for testing Jumo 213. Transferred to Tarnewitz April 1944.

Ta 153
First design, abandoned in favour of Ta 152 and this became the Fw 190D

Ta 152

V 33/U1	Works no. 0058, GH + KW, Jumo 213E-1, unarmed, prototype Ta 152H-O, total write-off 13.7.1944
V 30/U1	Works no. 0055, GH + KT, Jumo 213E-1 unarmed, prototype Ta 152H-O, total write-off 13.8.1944
V 29/U1	Works no. 0054, GH + KS, Jumo 213E-1. Maiden flight 23.9.1944. Prototype Ta 152H-O, 1 MK 108, 2 MG 151
V 32/U1	Works no. 0057, GH + KV, Jumo 213E-1. Still under test 17.12.1944 prototype Ta 152H-O
H-O	High altitude fighter, Jumo 213E-1; wing span 14.44 m; length 10.71 m; wing area 23.5 sq m; 1 MK 108, 2 MK 151/20, ETC 503B-1; 20 aircraft built starting November 1944
Fw 190 V 18/U1	Works no. 0040, similar to Ta 152H-O, but GM-1 and MW 50
V 25	Works no. 110025, similar to Fw 190 V18/U1, both prototypes for the Ta 152H-1
H-1	Similar to Ta 152H-O, FuG 16ZY and FuG 125
H-2	Similar to Ta 152H-1, but FuG 15 instead of FuG ZY and Jumo 213F engine. Project only
H-1/R11	All-weather fighter similar to Ta 152H-1, but Lgw K23 in addition. Only a few aircraft constructed
Fw 190 V 20/U1	Works no. 0043, GHK + KQ, DB 603 L, MK 108, 4 MG 151/20s, first flew October 1944, prototype for Ta 152B
V 19	Works No. 110019; wing span 11 m; 3 MK 103, first flew March 1945, prototype Ta 152B
B-5/R11	Similar to Ta 152 V19, FuG 16ZY and FuG 125, series production doubtful
FW 190 V 21/U1	Works no. 0044, GH + KR, DB 603 L, 1 MK 108, 4 MG 151/20; first flew November 1944, prototype for Ta 152C
V 6	Works no. 110006; produced 2.12.1944, first flew 28.2.1945, prototype for Ta 152-C-0/C-1, DB 603L

V 7	Works no. 110007, CI + XM, first flew December 1944, prototype for Ta 152C-0/R11; DB 603L
V 8	Works no. 110008, C1 + XN, prototypes Ta 152C-0/C-1/EZ
V 9 to V12	Cancelled
V 13	Works no. 110013, prototype Ta 152C-1, ready to fly December 1944
V 14	Cancelled
V 15	Works no. 110015, prototype Ta 152C-1, ready to fly February 1945
C-1	Small series constructed at Mitteldeutsche Metallwerke plant as C-1/R11 with FuG 125 and LGW K 23; DB 603L
C-2	Cancelled in favour of C-1
V 16	Works no. 110016, prototype C-3/R11, FuG 15, FuG 125, wing area 19.6 sq m
V 17	Works no. 110017, similar to V16, prototype C-3/R11; DB 603L
V 18	Works no. 110018, similar to V16, doubtful whether delivered
V 19 to V 25	Prototypes C-3 and C-4, doubtful whether built
V 26	Test airframe, not constructed
V 27	Works no. 150027; prototype for C-3/R11, 1 MK 103 and 4 MG 151
V 28	Works no. 150030; prototype C-3/R11, similar to V27
C-3/R11	Corresponding to V27/V28, only prototypes V22, V23 and V24. Doubtful whether constructed
V 9	Reconnaisance aircraft similar to Ta 152C-1, prototype for Ta 152E-1
V 14	Reconnaisance aircraft with obliquely mounted camera, prototype for Ta 152E-1/R1
E-1	Reconnaisance aircraft with Rb 17/30, Jumo 213E-1, 1 MK 108 and 2 MG 151. Not constructed, but converted from Ta 152H-1s
S-1	Two seater fighter trainer, not built

2. Plans for development of the Fw 190/Ta 152

Fw 190	Converted frtom Fw 190A: BMW 801D replaced with a Focke-Wulf 2-stage radial compressor jet engine. Jet exit under the fuselage. Two MG 17 and two MG 151/20, Maximum speed 466 mph – 1942
Fw 190	High altitude fighter with DB 603 and turbo-supercharger; four MG 151/20; (wing span 12.3 m; length 9.5 m; wing area 20.3 sq m)
Fw 190	High altitude fighter with DB 603G and double turbo-supercharger (wing span 14.4 m; length 11.4 m; wing area 34 sq m)
Fw 190	High altitude fighter with DB 603G and TKL 15, similar to its predecessor, but length 11.32 m
Fw 190	Jumo 222A/B, (wing span 10.50 m; length 11.47 m), two MG 131 and two MG 151/20. Maximum speed 435 mph
Fw 190	Similar design with Jumo 222C, calculated to attain 460 mph
Fw 190	High altitude fighter with BMW 802 (2400 PS), (wing span 13 m; length 11.15m; wing area 34.5 sq m)
Fw 190	High altitude fighter with BMW 803 (3900 PS), (wing span 13.2 m); length 13.8 m; wing area 35 sq m); both these BMW designs armed with four MG 151/20.
Fw 190	High altitude fighter with BMW 801D and turbocharger; two MG 151/20, four blade propeller, pressurised cockpit.
Ta 152	Jumo 222 A/B, (wing span 11.0 m; length 10.62 m; wing area 19.6 sq m), four MG 151/20, FuG 16Z-Y and FuG 25a.
Ta 152	Jumo 222E/F (wing span 11.0 m; length 10.67; wing area 19.6 sq m) four MG 151/20, FuG 16ZY and FuG 25a.
Fw 190	Towing either Gotha P.56 as parasite fighter, glider fuel tank or glider bomb. Also intended for Ta 152.
Fw 190	Towing Gotha P.57 *Gleitbombe* (glider bomb), similar to P.56
Fw 190	As control aircraft for *Mistel* (Beethoven) composite with unmanned converted Ju 88G or H packed with explosives. It was later planned to use the Ta 154 as the lower aircraft.

3. Fw 190/Ta 152 aircraft still in existence

Fw 190 A-8/R6	Works no. 733682, Biggin Hill England
Fw 190 A-6/R6	Works no. 550214, Saxonwold Museum, Johannesburg, South Africa
Fw 190A-8	Henlow, Bedfordshire, England
Fw 190A-8	T2-117, Smithsonian, Maryland, USA
Fw 190A-8	NC900A-8 No. 62, Musee de L'Air, Paris, France
Fw 190A-8	Zemun, Yugoslavia
Fw 190A	Military Museum, Belgrade, Yugoslavia
Fw 190F-8	Works no. 640069 and 931884, as T2-116 and FE 116, Smithsonian, Washington, USA
Fw 190G-3	FE 125, Smithsonian, Maryland, USA
Fw 190G-3	Works no. 160016, DN + FP, as FE 104,

	Smithsonian, Maryland, USA	Fw 190 A-8/R6	Works no. 733682, Imperial War Museum, London, England
Fw 190D-9	FE 121, Smithsonian, on loan to US Air Force Museum, Wright-Patterson AFB, USA	Fw 190 A-8/U1	Works no. 584219, St. Athan, Wales Great Britain
Fw 190D-9	Works no. 210079, Atlanta, Georgia, USA	Ta 152 H-1	Works no. 150003, FE 112, Smithsonian, Maryland, USA
Fw 190 D-12	David Kyle, Santa Barbara, California, USA		

The French air force flew the Fw 190A-9 for some years after the war, calling it the AAC6

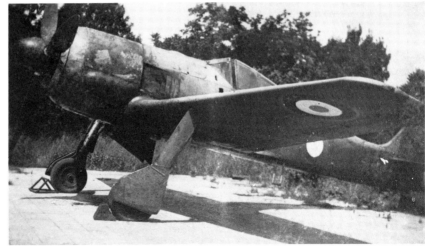

Later the AAC6 was renamed NC900. This aircraft was still on the edge of the airfield at Dijon in 1946.

Fw 190A-8/R6, works no. 733682 in the Imperial War Museum, London

151

Fw 190A-6/R6, works no. 550214 in Saxonwold
Museum, Johannesburg, South Africa

Fw 190D-9, works no. 601088 at the USAAF Museum,
Wright Patterson AFB, Dayton, Ohio, USA

Fw 190D-12 at Doug Camp Air Museum, Mesa,
Arizona, USA

Restored Fw 190F-8, works no. 640069 and 931884 in
the Smithsonian Institution, Washington, USA

4. Technical data for the main Fw 190 series

Aircraft Type	Fw 190 V1	A-1	A-3	A-5	A-6	A-8	F-2	F-8
Purpose	Test	Fighter	Fighter	Fighter	Ground Attack	Heavy Fighter	Ground Attack	Ground Attack
Crew	1	1	1	1	1	1	1	1
Engine	BMW 139	BMW 801C-1	BMW 801D	BMW 801D	BMW 801	BMW 801D	BMW 801D	BMW 801D
Power (PS)*	1550	1560	1770	1770	1770	1770	1770	1770
Wingspan (m)	9,515	10,383	10.506	10.383	10.506	10,506	10,383	10.506
Length (m)	8,85	8,85	8,798	8,95	8,95	8,95	8,95	8,95
Height	–	3,15	3,15	3,15	3,15	3,96	3,15	3,96
Wing area (m²)	14,9	18,3	18,3	18,3	18,3	18,3	18,3	18,3
Empty weight (kg)	–	2474	–	3141–3610	–	3170	–	–
All up weight (kg)	–	3400	–	3855–4650	4100	4400–4450	4533	4450
Maximum speed kph (mph)	–	590 (366)	–	656 (407)	651 (404)	644 (400)	–	620 (385)
Cruising speed kph (mph)	–	565 (351)	–	–	–	480 (304)	475 (295)	–
Range (miles)	–	621	–	931	838	931	–	745
Ceiling (ft)	21,320	21,320	24,600	34,400	33,950	32,640	–	–

*PS x 0.986 = BHP

Aircraft Type	Fw 190 G-1	G-3	G-8	D-9	D-11	Ta 152C	Ta 152H
	Long Range F/Bomber	Long Range F/Bomber	Long Range F/Bomber	Fighter	Fighter	Fighter	High Altitude Fighter
Crew	1	1	1	1	1	1	1
Engine	BMW 801D	BMW 801D	BMW 801D	Jumo 213A	Jumo 213F	DB 603LA	Jumo 213E
Power (PS)*	1770	1770	1770	1750	2060	2100	1730
Wingspan (m)	10,383	10,506	10,506	10.506	10.506	11,00	14,44
Length (m)	8,95	8,95	8,95	10,24	10,24	10,81	10,71
Height	3,15	3,36	3,36	3,36	3,36	3,38	3,36
Wing area (m²)	18,3	18,3	18,3	18,3	18,3	19,5	23,3
Empty weight (kg)	–	–	–	3490	–	4014	3920
All up weight (kg)	3900–4900	4100–4800	4000–5200	4270–4840	4509	5322	5220
Maximum speed kph (mph)	–	–	–	685 (425)	725 (450)	750 (465)	750 (465)
Cruising speed kph (mph)	450 (279)	460 (286)	450 (279)	–	–	520 (323)	500 (310)
Landing speed	–	–	–	–	–	174 (109)	155 (96)
Range (miles)	931	699	699	–	–	920	963
Ceiling (ft)	24,600	24,600	24,600	32,800	34,400	37,720	48,550

NB: Exact weight and performance details were unobtainable for the A F and G Series, but are probably similar to the A-5.

153

5. Armanent data for Fw 190 and Ta 152

	MG 17	MG 131	MG 151	MG 151/20	MG/FF	MK 103	MK 108	WGr 21
Calibre (mm)	7,92	13,1	15.1	20	20	30	30	210
Length (mm)	1175	1168	1917	1767	1338	2318	1057	1177
Height (mm)	159	123	195	195	135	348	216	–
Width (mm)	156	233	190	190	155	284	222	–
Barrel length (mm)	600	546	1250	1100	822	1338	550	–
Weight (kg)	10,2	19,7	41,5	42,3	35,7	145	58	111
Rounds per min	1200	930	700	720	540	420	650	1
Velocity (m/sec)	785	750	960	705	585	860	520	315

6. Field modification kits for the Fw 190/Ta 152

R 1: Only in the Fw 190A-4 and A-5. FuG 16Z-E installed.
R 1: Only in the A-6 to A-10. WB 151/20 weapon pod with two MG 151/20 slung under each wing.
R 2: As R 1 but a 3 cm MK 108 under each wing.
R 3: As R 2 but MK 103 instead of MK 108.
R 4: GM-1 emergency power boost injection system.
R 5: 115 litre auxiliary fuel tank in fuselage.
R 6: Two WGr 21 rocket launchers under the wings.
R 7: Additional armour for assault fighters.
R 8: Additional armour and two MK 108 under the wings.
R 11: FuG 125 and PKS 11, cockpit canopy heating for all-weather fighter.
R 12: As R 11, but in addition 2 MK 108 under the wings.

7. Fw 190/Ta 152 Power Plants

Bayerische Motorenwerke BMW 801 engine

The design of this 14 cylinder two-row radial engine was begun in October 1933 by a team under the direction of Dipl.-Ing Duckstein. The first engine was on the test bench as early as April 1939, and although it was obvious that it still had teething problems, the RLM released it for series construction in December 1939, with the result that the first series engines were supplied to aircraft factories in the middle of 1940. The Focke-Wulf Fw 190 V3 and V4 were two of the first aircraft to be powered by this engine.

It turned out that the designers had not succeeded in ensuring that the normal airflow to the cooling fins on the cylinders was adequate, although this had not been a problem with any of the foreign air-cooled double-row radial engines. The BMW 801 was the only engine of its type to require an additional cooling fan in front of the engine for adequate airflow for cooling. It became necessary to design a special control system for all the engine functions, this system being developed by Ing. Laibach to a design brief by Prestel. Sachse, the development director at BMW, presented this control system to representatives of the RLM and aircraft manufacturers in Berlin in 1939 and tried to justify the need for it, despite its not being necessary for any other engine of this type. There are numerous reports on the difficulties which this engine caused in operational use.

The first fighter version was the BMW 801C-0, but it was only with the advent of the BMW 801C-2 that the engine could be regarded as ready for series production. Development continued until 1942. The BMW 801D was developed from the BMW 801C-2 and was intended to improve the high altitude performance of the BMW 801. The BMW 801D-2 was the version produced in the largest numbers for fighters. Delays in the development of the BMW engine were caused by the RLM demanding the supply of the engine as a complete 'power egg'; this meant the engine itself with all auxiliary equipment such as the air cooling system with fan, ducts and seal rings had to be supplied, including the aerodynamic cowling and all fittings etc, ie, everything back to the attachment points on the fire wall. In addition the engine bearers and exhaust system were seen as part of the engine.

There was no doubt that the aircraft industry was not happy with the complicated cooling system and its control system. What they wanted was simply what other engine producers were able to provide, ie, a complete engine which they could install on a production line. A BMW 801TH engine intended for the Fw 190 was developed to production stage but not produced.

The following versions of the BMW 801 engine were developed and built for the Fw 190:

A   1600 PS, clockwise rotation, electrical propeller pitch adjustment, so called MA engine unit, series production 1039–43.
B   1600 PS like MA, but anti-clockwise, series discontinued.
C   1600 PS like A, but with hydraulic propeller pitch control.
D   1600 PS, project with single-stage 3-speed turbo-supercharger.
D-2 1730 PS, MG series engine, 1941–45, higher compression.
S-1 2200 PS similar to BMW 801E (2000 PS) prototype engine but with GM1 power boost injection for emergency high performance; standard production engine for the Fw 190 1944–45.
U-1 1730 PS similar to the D-2, standard fighter engine, 1944–45.

Although experiments had begun on the development of high altitude engines with exhaust driven turbo-superchargers as early as 1937, BMW did not succeed in developing a high altitude engine of this type.

Between 1940 and the end of the war a total of 21,000 BMW 801s were built. BMW achieved the highest production figures at the beginning of 1944 with 1,000 BMW 801s per month.

Daimler-Benz DB 603 engine

As early as the autumn of 1936 Daimler-Benz had offered this engine with a rated power of 1400-1500 PS to the RLM but had not obtained a contract to develop it – only an agreement that they could develop it at their own risk. In 1939 Daimler-Benz had an engine on the test bench which was already delivering 2800 PS. In 1937 the RLM had the development stopped, but then the situation changed and on 3 February 1940 an order was placed for 120 DB 603 engines. Series production began but the number required in 1941 could not be produced. The rated power was initially 1750 PS but in the course of development it was increased first to 1800, then 1900 and then 2000 PS. The DB 603A/D was series produced from 1942, the DB 603E from 1943 and the DB 603L from 1944. There were altogether over 36 different versions which varied only slightly from each other. The DB 603N was

not produced. The production of the DB 603U with exhaust turbo-supercharger failed through the lack of strategic materials already mentioned in the context of the construction of Fw 190C. The three main versions of this engine were as follows:

	DB 603A/D	DB 603E	DB 603L
Take-off power (PS)	1750	1800	2000
Climb/combat power (PS)	1510	1330	1510
rpm	2500	2500	2500
Rated altitude (ft)	18,700	24,275	30,175

Junkers Jumo 213 engine

This engine was one of the most powerful and was developed by a team led by Dr Ing. August Lichte at the Junkers-Motoren-Werken. Between the middle of 1942 and the end of the war in 1945 approximately 9,000 of this type were built. It was only supplied as a complete engine system and there were just two versions of it which offered different connections for the fire-proof bulkhead, to the dynamo drive, weapon synchronisation and cowling. The fighter engine, complete with Junkers variable pitch propeller such as fitted to the Fw 190 and Ta 152, weighed 1350 kg. Normal take-off power of the Jumo 213 was about 1750 PS but it could be increased for short periods to 2100 PS using the MW 50 emergency power boost system. Using special turbo-supercharging equipment it could produce 1900 PS for short periods at an altitude of 16,400 ft. In the Fw 190D-9 the MW 50 tank contained 115 litres of water/methanol which was adequate for 'emergency power' of 2100 PS for 40 minutes. There were the following versions of the Jumo 213:

A-1 1750 PS Two gear turbo-supercharger (series production August 1944).
AG   1900 PS special version.
B-0 2000 PS C-3 fuel (not series production).
C-0 1750 PS with cannon.
C-1 1750 PS series production from September 1944.
E-0 1870 PS high altitude engine.
E-1 1750 PS high altitude engine (series production 1944).
EB   2000 PS special version.
F   2050 PS high altitude engine (no series production).

The H, T and S versions did not advance beyond the project stage.

After the war, at Arsenal de L'Aeronautique in France, a project was developed to create a 24 cylinder H engine of 7200 PS using Jumo 213 parts. This development was cancelled in 1950.

8. Fw 190/Ta 152 Radio Equipment

Fw 190s series A-1 to A-3 were fitted wth FuG VIIa and FuG 25 short-wave radio equipment as standard. As the FuG 25 never saw service (except for a few in Berlin) the FuG 25A *Erstling* (first-born) was fitted from 1943. This was used on the western front, and over Germany in the 'Egon' fighter command system for example. It is likely that the Fw 190s around the English Channel which used the FuG VIIa for the fighter direction finding system were fitted with electrical remote selection of two frequencies and with a modulation unit from the summer of 1940 onwards. In bad weather or if forced to ditch, the fighter pilot could transmit location signals on the second frequency and be located by the direction finding system, so that the rescue boats would then know where to look for him.

The first FuG 25A *Erstling* prototypes were delivered by the firm GEMA starting in 1941. In the summer of 1942 the first pre-series units were available and they were successfully tested by JG 2 in the English Channel coastal area under operational conditions.

In the *Erstling* system a *Freya* (goddess) radar unit detected the enemy. At the same time a *Freya* or *Würzburg-Riese* (Würzburg giant) direction finder with the *Kuh* (cow) transmitter and *Gemse* (chamois) receiver would locate the fighter in terms of distance and direction and then the necessary course correction would be told to the pilot over the radio. From 1943 onward the series production equipment was available and was fitted to aircraft in the West, later also those over Germany, so that ground radar would differentiate between German and enemy aircraft.

As far as it is known all the Fw 190A-4s were equipped wth FuG 16Z and the FuG 25 or FuG25a modification kit. The change from FuG 25 to FuG25a occurred in the middle of series production. Originally a T-shaped wire aerial was fitted to the small aerial mast on the fin but this was then replaced by a homing device frame antenna mounted across the airflow underneath the fuselage.

From the spring of 1943 some of the Fw 190A-4s in

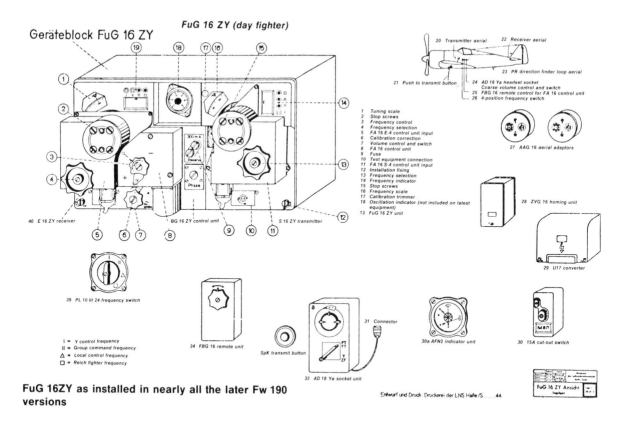

FuG 16ZY as installed in nearly all the later Fw 190 versions

service with the SKG 10 on the English Channel were, in addition to the FuG 167, also equipped with modulation unit, remote frequency selection (for 2 and later 4 frequencies) and timer switch for the fighter direction system.

After many weeks of daylight attacks there was a switch to night attacks and in this case the lead aircraft transmitted a locating signal for 15 seconds on demand. In Cassel and Poix the VHF locating units communicated the location of the formation and transmitted to them the course and their distance from target on two-way radio, but without switching as was later used in the FuG 16ZE and ZY. When returning to base the radio communication was again on one frequency. Accordingly, the SKG10 aircraft had to have a second aerial under the fuselage.

For a time JG1 introduced a so-called *Peilruf-Verfahren (Jagd)* direction finding system for fighters. The FuG 16Z time switch in the lead aircraft switched to a second frequency for 20 seconds every two minutes and transmitted a tone modulated identification as its locating signal. Three location stations on the ground then communicated their location and appropriate commands for course and height to bring them into contact with the enemy formations identified by radar.

As the 'Y' fighter command system (daytime) was first used in the field by II/JG1 in the Holland/Ruhr area from August 1942 it is probable that Fw 190A-4/R1 lead aircraft, equipped with FuG 16ZE would have been used. In fact these ZE units were not capable of direction finding and if the direction finding loop aerial was damaged it was not unusual for it not to be replaced. Initially the Fw 190A-4/R1 was therefore purely a marker aircraft. It received the ground station tone (transmitted for 5 seconds every 20 seconds) and transmitted it back to the ground station on a different frequency (ie a sort of transponder system). This meant that a second aerial was necessary. The frequency allocation in use meant that the ground station could only hear air-to-air communications via the lead aircraft's equipment. It meant that it was necessary for each of the other aircraft acting as marker aircraft to have the FuG 16ZE using frequency switching. Later the wing man of the formation leader was used as marker aircraft which was better for commanding larger formations.

In the Fw 190A-4 the FuG 16Z or ZE was mounted facing sideways on the cockpit wall at the side of the pilot, just as the FuG VIIa had been in the case of the A-1, A-2 and A-3. It was only from the A-8 that FuG 16ZY was installed behind and facing forwards. The FuG 16ZE was really only an emergency aid as it was ineffective as homing function, so at the beginn-

ing of 1942 the firm of Lorenz received a contract to design and build a new and effective homing device. This was the FuG 16ZY which was supplied from April 1943. The firm achieved a monthly output of 7000 of these units so that from about the middle of July 1943 all Fw 190s (and Me 109s) were equipped with FuG 16ZY.

The 'Y' system made very great demands on the ground station services so by Autumn 1944 there were 500 'Y' ground stations in operation. In the Spring of 1944 introduction of the new 'EGON' system (EGON = *Erstling Gemse* – Offensive-Navigation) began. It was a remote command system suggested by the Rechlin test centre. The ground based fighter command equipment was a modified *Freya* radar unit transmitting on 125 MHz and receiving FuG 25a identification signals on 156 MHz. From August 1944 in the north west area and in Austria about a dozen fighter control stations had the additional benefit of the 'EGON' system. The Fug 25A *Hermine* was intended for single seat all weather fighter formations for navigation using the *Hermes* (Mercury) VHF radio beacons and for using the VHF fighter landing aids, both in the 30.0-33.3 MHz range. In January 1945 there were five *Hermes* beacons ready for service. It is believed that by April more than about 13 or 14 would have been set up across Germany.

Although the FuG 125 was fully developed by the middle of 1944 its manufacture was delayed by the low priority attached to individual components with the result that by the end of the war there were very few aircraft, most of them Ta 152s, which were equipped with it. It is believed that a few Fw 190A-8/R11s also had this unit.

The FuG 217 J1 *Neptun F1* was developed by the Flugfunkforschungsinstitut Oberpfaffenhofen (Aviation Radio Research Institute) and built by the firm of Seibt. It was only produced in small numbers and installed in a few Fw 190A-6s. It was superceded by the Siemens-developed FuG 218 V1 *Neptun III V1* which by the end of the war had only been produced as a small pre-series and fitted in a few Fw 190A-8/R11s.

There was an FuG 15 which was originally meant to supercede the FuG 16 and FuG 17 units but it was not suitable for use with the 'Y' system and so was only produced as a short run of 40.

The FuG 17, mentioned in connection with the Fw 190A-4 and A-4/U4 was largely similar to the FuG 16 and differed only in detail.

9. Fw 190 and Ta 152 Works Numbers

Production of the Fw 190 was identified by blocks of serial numbers which were allocated to the Focke-

Wulf factory in Bremen and their dispersed factories and sub-contractors. This is in line with the general system throughout the German aircraft industry from 1935 to 1945. However, whereas most other manufacturers identify the airframe with the full works number, Focke-Wulf simple identified it by the last three numbers of the serial block. The complete serial number was only to be found inside the aircraft, in the cockpit. That is why it is often not possible to establish the exact works number when only photos of an aircraft are available. It is easier, of course, in the case of aircraft captured by the Allies and aircraft whose exact works number can be confirmed through log books and airfield logs. Thanks to years of intensive research work by individual enthusiasts such as Rainer Haufschild, Volker Bünz and others, it has gradually become possible to get a clear view of the individual serial number blocks of the Fw 190

series. Unfortunately, this research does not include information on which serial numbers were allocated to which factories.

It is even more difficult in the case of the Ta 152 because old Fw 190A-0s were first converted to Fw 190Cs and then to prototypes of the Ta 152. On the other hand Ta 152 prototype aircraft were built which bore numbers from the Ta 152 serial blocks 110 and 150. It would appear that these serial blocks where allocated to the Focke-Wulf factories in Kottbus and Sorau. It follows that, for example, works number 170003, although it was first a prototype for the D9 series, was given the designation Fw 190 V53, but was also converted to the Fw 190 V68, which became the prototype of the Ta 152B. It was originally an Fw 190A-8 which can be seen clearly from the serial block arrangement for the individual series. The following is a list of the Fw 190 serial block numbers:

Fw 190A-1	0110001-102	670 000	682 000	**Fw 190A-9** 200 000
Fw 190A-2	0120 201	(only a few)	(also a few	201 000
	0122 000		A-9s)	202 000
	0125 000	**Fw 190A-7** 340 000	683 000	203 000
Fw 190A-3	0130 000	430 000	688 000	205 000
	0132 000	431 000	690 000	206 000
	0135 000	432 000	(also a few	207 000
	0137 000	540 000	A-9s)	209 000
		640 000	730 000	380 000
Fw 190A-4	0140 000	642 000	731 000	(also A-8)
	0142 000	643 000	732 000	690 000
	0145 000		733 000	(also A-8)
	0147 000	**Fw 190A-8** 170 000	734 000	750 000
Fw 190A-5	0150 000	171 000	737 000	910 000
	0151 000	172 000	738 000	980 000
	0152 000	173 000	739 000	
	0155 000	174 000	960 000	
	0157 000	175 000	961 000	
	(0158 000?)	176 000	(a few	
		177 000	Fw 190A-9s)	
Fw 190A-5	150 000	178 000		
	155 000	179 000		
	160 000	350 000		
	180 000	352 000		
	410 000	380 000		
	500 000	(in this block		
	505 000	there are also		
	710 000	A-9s)		
	840 000	490 000		
		580 000		
Fw 190A-6	470 000	581 000		
	530 000	(650 000?)		
	531 000	(670 000?)		
	550 000	680 000		
	551 000	681 000		

Bibliography

Aders: The Focke-Wulf 190 (from the Journal "Luftfahrt International" 1981). (No longer published).

Angelucci: Flugzeuge, Stuttgart 1974

Chant: II. Weltkriegsflugzeuge, Bonn 1976.

Coffey: Entscheidung über Schweinfurt, Berlin 1977.

Dierich: Die Verbände der Luftwaffe 1935-45, Stuttgart 1976.

Gersdorff/Grasmann: Flugmotoren und Strahltriebwerke, Munich 1981.

Hahn: Deutsche Geheimwaffen 1939-45, Heidenheim 1963.

Kens/Nowarra: Die deutschen Flugzeuge 1933-45, 5th edition, Munich 1977.

Nowarra: The Focke-Wulf 190, a Famous German Fighter, Letchworth, Herts 1965.

Nowarra: Udet – Vom Fliegen besessen, Friedberg 1981.

Obermaier: Die Ritterkreuzträger der Luftwaffe (Jagdflieger), Mainz 1966.

Sims: Jagdflieger, Stuttgart, 1980.

Trenkle: Die deutschen Funk-Navigations-und Funkführungsverfahren, Stuttgart, 1979.

Trenkle: Die deutschen Funklenkverfahren, Ulm 1982.

Weber/Feist: Focke-Wulf 190, Fallbrook, CA, USA 1968.

Thetford/Riding: Aircraft of the Fighting Powers, Leicester, England 1942-46.

Focke-Wulf works archives 1939-45, MBB Bremen.

A-1-2 (G) Report Ro. 2383 (USA), German Aircraft, new and projected types, US Air Force 1946.

Kriegstagebuch des Oberkommandos der Wehrmacht 1940 bis 1945, Herrsching 1982.

Airfield Operations Register: Langenhagen 2 June 1944 to 6 April 1945.